GROUP THERAPY

DEFENSE MECHANISMS

Suzanne M. Howard
Board Certified Mental Health Coach,
AACC

Battle Press
SATELLITE BEACH, FLORIDA

Group Therapy
Defense Mechanisms

Copyright © 2023 by Suzanne M. Howard

Books may be ordered through booksellers or by contacting:

Suzanne M. Howard
suzhoward@yahoo.com
www.suzannemhoward.com

Or

Battle Press
steve@battlepress.media
battlepress.media
919-218-4039

Because of the dynamic nature of the internet, any web addresses or links contained in this book may have changed since publication and may no longer be valid.

ISBN: 979-8-9873-3793-6 (SC)
ASIN: B0BRT8X6LY (eBook)

First Edition.

TABLE OF CONTENTS

DEDICATION

This book is dedicated to Audrea Holley "Tangie", DeMechia "Mechia" Wilson, and Leah "LeeLee" Shaw.

Thank you for everything! Words couldn't cover it all, thank you for all that you have given me in love and support.

ABOUT THE AUTHOR

Suzanne M. Howard is a Certified Mental Health Coach, speaker, Pastor and Author of Group Therapy, Self, a series of self-help and personal development books. She is also founder of suzannemhoward.com Coaching.

Suzanne has over a decade of writing curriculums and sermons and speaking throughout the New England region and beyond. She has turned a personal journey into a much broader influence of helping others through their journey. Being a teenage mother, Suzanne has fought, failed, and won many battles. She is devoted to her faith and her lifelong mission to help others overcome their soul issues. She resides in Connecticut with her husband, son, and granddaughter.

Suzanne is available for group workshops and one-on-one coaching or mentoring sessions. To learn more please check her out at:

suzannemhoward.com

psychologytoday.com

INTRODUCTION

Whether you know it or not, you are most likely in a constant battle with your defenses. We all are. Day to day we battle with reality: How we can cope, and what level of effort is needed to survive given current circumstances? We wrestle with ourselves and reality is our opponent.

Defense Mechanisms are necessary and useful to every human being on this planet. If we did not possess the ability, we would not survive. Even persistent and overly protective defenses indicate resiliency, often left-overs from troublesome life experiences

Like the notion of an unconscious mind, the idea of defense mechanisms has entered the mainstream and colored our understanding of human nature. Nearly everyone understands what it means to appear defensive or to react defensively.

We owe this understanding of defensiveness to the earliest work of Sigmund Freud. Freud began writing about the concept of defense mechanisms in the 1890s, most notably in his famous early work, Studies on Hysteria which he co-authored with Josef Breuer.

Freud wrote in German, of course, and the word he used to describe this mental phenomenon was abwehr, more accurately translated as a "warding off" or "fending off" rather than "defense". Freud's idea is a simple one, and not as machine-like as the unfortunate English term defense mechanisms make it sound. According to Freud, sometimes when we're confronted with an idea or feeling that we find too painful or morally unacceptable, we ward it off, pushing it into the unconscious. It's not a deliberate decision; it happens outside of awareness, in ways that are often automatic.

This basic idea of the nature and function of defense mechanisms is widely accepted by most psycho-dynamic thinkers and therapists today. This view of the nature and function of defense mechanisms makes it easier to connect them to our personal experience. Everyone can sympathize with the desire to avoid pain.

We all understand how easy it is to deceive ourselves when facing the truth will hurt badly or make it difficult to function. Sometimes, our defense mechanisms help us to get by when facing the full truth would render life unbearable. At other times, however, we need to confront our pain; avoiding the truth feels better for the moment, but it might only make matters worse in the long run. Here's an example using one of the most common defense mechanisms, one that everyone understands: to be in denial about your spouse's affair (when the tell-tale signs are obvious) might help you avoid feeling the pain of betrayal, but it prevents you from dealing with this catastrophe in your life and all the collateral damage - to your children, your friendships, your feelings of self-worth.

Defense mechanisms operate in the here and now, with no thought for tomorrow. They're unthinking and reflexive; they aim only to ward off pain this very moment and don't take into account the long-term costs of doing so. Sometimes we eventually "wake up" and face the truth. Sometimes unconscious knowledge breaks through and we realize what has been brewing unnoticed within us for a long time. More often, we continue as we were, our defense mechanisms in place and unnoticed. Human beings are creatures of habit and change is difficult.

.

CHAPTER ONE
WHAT IS DEFENSE MECHANISM?

Defense mechanism is a way for the mind to protect us from being consciously aware of thoughts or feelings that are too difficult to tolerate. In other words, it allows the unconscious thought, feeling or fears to be expressed indirectly in some type of disguised form.

Defense mechanisms are mental operations that disguise or otherwise modify the content of the mind and/or the perception of reality. The purpose of these mental functions is to protect the individual from being disturbed by excessively painful feelings, drives (motives), or ideas. The operation of defense mechanisms is generally unconscious – that is unknown to the individual – for the function of disguise is effective only if the individual is unaware of the deception. Because of the distortions involved, the operation of defense mechanisms may interfere with the veracity of the individual's view of internal or external reality.

Defense mechanisms are patterns of feelings, thoughts, or behaviors that are relatively involuntary. They arise in response to perceptions of psychic danger or conflict, to unexpected changes in the internal or external environment, or in response to cognitive dissonance.

Defense mechanisms can restore psychological homeostasis by ignoring or deflecting sudden increases in impulse, affect, and emotion. Defense mechanisms can provide a mental time-out to adjust to sudden changes in reality or self-image. Defenses can mitigate sudden unresolvable conflict with important people, living or dead. Finally, defenses can mitigate conflict due to social learning or conscience.

Sigmund Freud popularized the concept of human defense mechanisms when he introduced his personality model—the id, ego, and superego.

- The id houses basic needs, impulses, and desires. Simply, the id acts as a hedonistic pleasure center whose primary goal is to satisfy basic needs and drives.

- The ego is responsible for how we react to, function in, and make sense of the external world. The ego controls the demands of impulses of the id and is home to our consciousness.

- The superego houses all the rules that we have learned throughout our life and uses these to control the ego. The superego is also home to the expectations of the ego: the way we should behave and think.

Ideally, the id, ego, and superego interact in concert and harmoniously. However, each component can cause anxiety within an individual.

Sigmund Freud argued that when placed in a psychologically dangerous or threatening situation, the patient was likely to resort to defense mechanisms for protection. In a psychoanalytic context, a dangerous threat is something that challenges the patient's self-concept or self-esteem.

DEFENSE MECHANISM VS COPING MECHANISM

Defense mechanisms and coping mechanisms are discussed as two different types of adaptational processes. They may be differentiated based on the psychological processes involved, but not based on their relation to outcome measures.

Usually, defense mechanisms may be defined as a mechanism that is used unconsciously at a subconscious level when a person encounters a threat in their environment. This threat may be external or internal. Examples of external threats may be a physical danger that invokes a fight or flight response in any individual or internal threats such as panic.

On the other hand, coping mechanisms are mechanisms used by any individual on a conscious level to deal with an external or internal threat present in their environment. Therefore, the significant difference between coping and defense mechanisms can be described as different levels of processing of the said threat, with defense at a subconscious level and coping at a conscious level.

In today's world, knowing what coping mechanisms are of great use. Why do we say this? It is simply because we are living in a world full of intricacies and complexities. It is rather obvious that not only collectively but individually too our lives have become rather complex. People deal with a strict schedule and are pressed with work. This creates a lot of stress and tension even within the daily routine. Coping mechanism contributes towards reducing this stress and tension through different coping strategies. Stress can be both positive and negative. It is usually a response to change. Coping mechanisms help people to adjust to such situations without risking the well-being of the individual.

Further, we can also go ahead and suggest that the ability to cope is a form of defense mechanism that places after an environmental threat has been detected and assessed. Following the assessment, a coping decision has to be taken by the individual undertaken by the threat to deal with it with resilience and efficiency.

Defense mechanisms, on the other hand, deal with threats at a subconscious level and therefore, cannot be assessed beforehand. As a result of this, they are a result of an immediate action taken by the brain to protect the body at large from the threat.

Adaptive & Maladaptive Coping Mechanisms

There are two types of coping mechanisms: Adaptive (healthy) and maladaptive (unhealthy). Finding ways to cope can be stressful in itself, as the stress can often cloud one's judgment on the best way to handle these stressors and challenging emotions. This may lead to adopting maladaptive patterns of coping, but with the right tools in place before a stressor hits, utilizing adaptive strategies is the best path forward.

Adaptive Coping Mechanisms

Adaptive coping mechanisms are positive and life-enhancing ways of dealing with stressors. These are healthier coping mechanisms that support your life and the direction you want to go when dealing with stress. Those who choose adaptive coping mechanisms tend to have a positive outlook and can strengthen their mental health, even if they have a history of mental health issues. Dealing with these challenges head-on builds self-confidence and self-esteem so that an individual can handle these life stressors healthily.

Maladaptive Coping Mechanisms

Maladaptive coping mechanisms, such as avoidance coping, are harmful and generally can cause more stress and difficult emotions as a result. Maladaptive coping means participating in activities that are counterproductive and can worsen existing feelings of stress. The immediate effects of maladaptive coping can appear to be helpful, which is why many people engage in this way of coping, however, in the long term, individuals are left feeling worse. Examples of maladaptive coping mechanisms are heavy drinking and drug use, gambling, impulsivity, and other risky or self-harm behaviors.

When individuals choose maladaptive coping mechanisms, they tend to have a more grim outlook as their choice of coping includes something that can further worsen their feelings long-term. This way of coping highlights how individuals who choose maladaptive coping mechanisms may be trying to avoid and numb the stressful issues they are facing. By not taking a head-on approach, the patterns of processing feelings and moving past them become delayed or avoided, and over time, those emotions multiply—creating even more challenging experiences related to existing stressors.

A few examples of defense mechanism can be a rationalization, for example, rationalizing your way out of a difficult situation, a project wherein a person usually projects their insecurities onto another person because they feel attacked for their choices at a deeper level, a displacement which suggests displacing the anxiety produced by the said threat onto different areas which may also result in using an avoidance approach to not indulge with the threat, denial where the person denials dealing with the threat altogether, repression where an individual tries to repress incidents or memories that can produce intense uncomfortable emotions and many more.

Coping, on the other hand, takes place consciously, and thus, the person diving into a coping mechanism makes conscious decisions that may be good or bad to deal with their environmental threat. Bad coping takes place when mechanisms such as drug abuse, smoking, drinking, and similar bad behaviors are undertaken by the person suffering from a threat and as a result, uses a mechanism that is denial or repression-focused.

These behaviors may provide a likely relief to the person, for example, smoking a cigarette, but leaves long-term counter effects on the body and brain of the person which can later prove to be fatal for the said individual. Whereas good coping mechanisms can be described as conscious decisions that are undertaken by any individual to deal with the environmental threat positively and healthily.

A few examples of good coping behavior may be, reassessing your expectations and lowering them to be more realistic about a particular situation, seeking help from professionals or peers to better deal with the situation, engaging yourself in a problem-solving approach rather than a problem-focused approach wherein you focus on curating solutions for the threat, finding alternative remedies for the threat to relive frustration such as exercising, journalizing or meditating and many more counter-effective remedies.

To sum up, everything that has been said so far, we may conclude that defense mechanisms and coping mechanisms often meet at an intersection wherein coping mechanisms can be considered a conscious decision after realizing that unconscious defense mechanisms are at play.

These mechanisms are used by the human body as a signal identifying the threat at large which may affect the individual's functioning in everyday life if not dealt with. As a result of this, it may be a benefit for the person experiencing the threat to evaluate the defense mechanism being used subconsciously and based on that formulate a coping strategy to deal with that particular threat to living their best life.

WHY DO WE FORM DEFENSE MECHANISM?

Our addictions and mental health issues bring along with them all kinds of coping mechanisms and defense mechanisms, many of which we engage in compulsively and by default but without realizing we're doing them. We might not be aware of them until someone brings them to our attention. We might continue them for years, even for most of our lives, without being aware of them. Some of us will instinctively use denial, avoidance, secrecy, dishonesty, control, or manipulation, either within ourselves or with the people in our lives. We might do things we regret but feel powerless to stop. It can be extremely difficult to feel as though we lack understanding around our defense mechanisms, and part of the work we'll have to do to recover will entail becoming more mindful of our defense mechanisms and working to understand why we've developed them in the first place to figure out how to shed them.

The majority of our behaviors are governed by the subconscious mind. This means that what we think and feel subconscious has a great deal of power over our behavioral patterns, including our defense mechanisms.

For many of us, we're subconsciously trying to protect ourselves, from being hurt, judged, rejected, feeling unloved, and abandoned. We're trying to protect ourselves from losing people, from feeling the grief and pain of loss. We're trying to protect ourselves from the consequences we think we'll suffer if we lose control, autonomy, and authority, within the situations in our lives and our relationships, and within ourselves. We're afraid of feeling our pain and having to address our deeply rooted issues without anything to numb them or distract us from them. We're afraid of living life without our drugs of choice.

Our defense mechanisms become our default, go-to methods of coping with pain and trying to protect ourselves. They often develop after intense traumatic experiences that are destabilizing and that create a foundation of fear within us, a foundation from which we build our fear-based responses, act on our fears, and live out our fears. If we were emotionally neglected as children, for example, we might start to use manipulation and dishonesty in our relationships to prevent ourselves from ever feeling neglected again. We might subconsciously believe that if we shield ourselves from vulnerability by being manipulative and dishonest, we'll never again have to experience the deep, traumatic pain of neglect.

Our defense mechanisms don't help us heal, they don't keep us safe, and they don't protect us from harm. Because they are rooted in our pain, they usually work against us and compound our many issues, creating more suffering for us to have to contend with. Our recovery from addiction and mental illness involves working to understand and then dismantle the defense mechanisms that have been holding us back and preventing our healing.

HOW DOES DEFENSE MECHANISM WORK?

As human beings, we are designed to protect ourselves from danger. Our will to survive is primal and innate, but it isn't limited to physical threats to our life. From the time we are born, we develop strategies to cope with unfavorable circumstances. As infants, we learn the best techniques to get our needs met by our parents, and as we grow up, we make adaptations to help us endure pain, be it psychological or existential.

Early in our lives, our defense mechanisms can feel like tools for our very survival. However, as we grow up, these same psychological defenses can start to hurt rather than help us. Because of this, getting to know each defense mechanism we've formed can serve the deeper purpose of helping us break free of self-imposed limitations. By recognizing and shedding our outdated defense mechanisms, we can develop within ourselves, form deeper relationships, and start to live a life that looks more like the one we desire and less like the one we were prescribed by our past.

A defense can operate very much like the antiquated armor we wear with the hope of protecting ourselves, but instead, it limits our mobility and shuts out much more than we imagine. Ironically, our defense mechanisms can do a lot more damage than good when it comes to the quality of our lives.

Defense mechanisms are ways you react to situations that bring up negative emotions. According to the psychoanalytic theory rested Source, when you experience a stressor, the subconscious will first monitor the situation to see if it might harm you. If the subconscious believes the situation might lead to emotional harm, it may react with a defense mechanism to protect you.

Usually, you are unaware of the defense mechanism, though the behavior may appear odd to others around you.

Many researchers trusted Source place defense mechanisms on a continuum, with more mature defenses improving cognitive processes and less mature ones causing harm. In the long term, mature defense mechanisms may not be particularly detrimental to your emotional or mental health. Using more mature mechanisms may help you face the anxieties and situations that might normally cause stress and emotional duress.

Other defense mechanisms, however, are not as mature and helpful. Prolonged use of these defenses can lead to lingering problems. They may prevent you from ever facing emotional issues or anxieties because they block you from seeing the root cause.

Some signs that defense mechanisms are getting in the way of your everyday life and mental health may include:

- Feeling sad or depressed

- Having difficulty getting out of bed

- Avoiding usual daily activities, things, or people that once made you happy

- Having difficulty forming or maintaining healthy relationships

- Communication problems that hinder your professional or personal life.

.

CHAPTER TWO
TYPES OF DEFENSE MECHANISM

We all use defense mechanisms. Many of us may not even realize that we are using them. A defense mechanism is an unconscious psychological tool people use to avoid unpleasant feelings, such as anxiety. Defense mechanisms take many forms, and learning whether you use any of them is an important part of your recovery journey and overall well-being. Once we realize we do something, we can learn how it affects our lives.

It's human instinct to protect ourselves. We often put up defenses to shield ourselves from painful realities, especially during active addiction. In recovery, we use defenses, too, when we're hiding from our true selves or trying to prevent others from getting close to us. We use defenses when we don't want to face our feelings or the real motivations behind our behavior.

While defenses can help us avoid pain, they do so in an unhealthy way. If we rely on our defenses too often, we distort our reality so much that it becomes dangerous. When the facade comes crashing down or becomes too much to bear, it's easy to relapse.

We must learn to identify our defenses. Most of us rely on one or two main types of defenses. If we can recognize when we're using them, we can force ourselves to confront our feelings head-on, which helps maintain the emotional sobriety we need to stay clean.

For many of us, any situation that brings uncertainty triggers an unconscious protective measure that allows us to cope with unpleasant emotions. Sometimes tapping into defense mechanisms can be useful; it helps us avoid dwelling on or doing something with potentially damaging ramifications. We keep ourselves in a better state – at least in the short term.

Yet in the long run, the effect of these defense mechanisms is the opposite. Due to defense mechanisms psychology, when we routinely employ our defenses, it can reduce the effectiveness of our emotional processing. We begin to feel as if we are not in charge of our own emotions, which prevents us from working through issues.

This is why it is key to become more cognizant of your tendencies so you don't let your defense mechanisms overtake your progress in life. How do you handle stressful situations? Do you live in a state of denial when bad news comes your way? Do you find yourself constantly making excuses for your behavior? These are just a few common defense mechanism examples that can limit your progress if you aren't aware of them.

As you create a defense mechanism definition that resonates with you, understand that types of defense mechanisms range from shifting blame to shutting down. Though each person has their own unique defense mechanism examples, most of the mechanisms themselves are common and easy to spot.

1. Denial

Denial is an ego defense mechanism that operates unconsciously to resolve emotional conflict and to reduce anxiety by refusing to perceive the more unpleasant aspects of external reality.

Denial is being used in a situation in which a person faced with a fact that is uncomfortable or painful to accept rejects it, instead insisting that it is not true, despite what may be overwhelming evidence. The subject may deny the reality of the unpleasant fact altogether (simple denial), admit the fact but deny its seriousness (minimization), or admit both the fact and seriousness but deny responsibility (transference). The concept of denial is particularly important to the study of addiction.

The theory of denial was first researched seriously by Anna Freud. She classified denial as a mechanism of the immature mind because it conflicts with the ability to learn from and cope with reality. Where denial occurs in mature people, it is most often associated with death and dying. Research in this area has significantly expanded the scope and utility of the concept. Elisabeth Kübler-Ross used denial as the first of five stages in the psychology of a dying patient, and the idea has been extended to include the reactions of survivors to news of a death. Thus, when parents are informed of the death of a child, their first reaction is often of the form, "No! You must have the wrong house, you can't mean our child!"

Unlike some defense mechanisms postulated by psychoanalytic theory (for instance, repression), the general existence of denial is fairly easy to verify, even for non-specialists. On the other hand, denial is one of the most controversial defense mechanisms, since it can be easily used to create unfalsifiable theories: anything the subject says or does that appears to disprove the interpreter's theory is explained, not as evidence that the interpreter's theory is wrong, but as evidence of the subject's being "in denial."

The concept of denial is important in "twelve-step" programs, where the abandonment or reversal of denial forms the basis of the first, fourth, fifth, eighth, and tenth steps. The ability to deny or minimize is an essential part of what enables an addict to continue his or her behavior in the face of evidence that, to an outsider, appears overwhelming. This is cited as one of the reasons that compulsion is seldom effective in treating addiction—the habit of denial remains.

Understanding and avoiding denial is also important in the treatment of various diseases. The American Heart Association cites denial as a principal reason that treatment of a heart attack is delayed. Because the symptoms are so varied, and often have other potential explanations, the opportunity exists for the patient to deny the emergency, often with fatal consequences. It is common for patients to delay mammograms or other tests because of a fear of cancer, even though this is maladaptive. It is the responsibility of the care team, and the nursing staff, in particular, to train at-risk patients to avoid such behavior.

2. Repression/Suppression

Repression and suppression are very similar defense mechanisms. They both involve a process of pulling thoughts into the unconscious and preventing painful or dangerous thoughts from entering consciousness. The difference is that repression is an unconscious force, while suppression is a conscious process, a conscious choice not to think about something.

Repression can often be detrimental. Suppression, however, is entirely conscious and thus can be managed. Because repression is unconscious, it manifests itself through a symptom, or series of symptoms sometimes called the "return of the repressed." A repressed sexual desire, for example, might resurface in the form of a nervous cough or a slip of the tongue. In this way, although the subject is not conscious of the desire and so cannot speak it out loud, the subject's body can still articulate the forbidden desire through the symptom.

It has often been claimed that traumatic events are "repressed," yet it appears that it is more likely that the occurrence of these events is remembered in a distorted manner. One problem from an objective research point of view with this situation is that a "memory" is usually defined as what someone says or does. It cannot be measured or recorded objectively since there is no way to verify the existence and/or accuracy of memory except through its correspondence to some other, independent representation of past events (written records, photographs; reports of others, etc).

Normal repression in psychoanalytic theory is considered to have two stages, which are progressively involved in the creation of the individual's sense of "self" and "other," of "good" and "bad," and of the aspects of personality called "ego" and "superego."

In the Primary Repression phase, the infant learns that some aspects of reality are pleasant, and others are unpleasant; that some are controllable, and others not. To define the "self," the infant must repress the natural assumption that all things are equal. Primary repression, then, is the process of determining what is self, what is other, what is good, and what is bad. Once done, the child can then distinguish between desires, fears, self, and mother/other.

Secondary Repression begins once the child realizes that acting on some desires may evoke anxiety. For example, the child who desires the mother's breast may be denied and feel threatened with punishment, perhaps by the father. This anxiety leads to repression of the desire for the mother's breast. The threat of punishment related to this form of anxiety when internalized becomes the "superego," which intercedes against the desires of the "ego" without the need for any identifiable external threat.

Abnormal repression, or complex, neurotic behavior involving repression and the superego, occurs when repression develops or continues to develop due to the internalized feelings of anxiety, in ways leading to behavior that is illogical, self-destructive, or anti-social. A psychotherapist may try to reduce this behavior by revealing and re-introducing the repressed aspects of the patient's mental process to his conscious awareness, and then teaching the patient how to reduce any anxieties felt about these feelings and impulses.

Suppression generally has more positive results than repression. First of all, it deals with unpleasant but not despicable actions or thoughts. It is maybe even useful and rational to focus on one thing at a time, suppressing other problems until that one is solved. Counting to ten when angry—before taking action—is not only an example of suppression, but it is also a technique very useful in everyday life.

The problem with repression is that whatever we are trying to push away into the subconscious is not lost. The subconscious tends to empower it, and the more one tries to repress something, the more powerful and attractive it becomes. Finally, the repressed desire starts to manifest itself in actions, often in ways not noticeable to the person repressing it, but noticeable to others.

3. Projection

Projection can be defined as attributing to others one's own unacceptable or unwanted thoughts and/or emotions. Projection reduces anxiety in the way that it allows the expression of the impulse or desire, without letting the ego recognize it.

This defense mechanism "projects" one's undesirable thoughts, motivations, desires, and feelings—parts of oneself—onto someone else (usually another person, but psychological projection onto animals and inanimate objects also occur).

To understand the process, imagine an individual (Alice, for example) who feels dislike for another person (let's say Bob), but whose unconscious mind will not allow her to become aware of this negative emotion. Instead of admitting to herself that she feels dislike for Bob, she projects her dislike onto Bob, so that her conscious thought is not "I don't like Bob," but rather "Bob doesn't like me." In this way, one can see that projection is related to denial, the only defense mechanism that is considered more primitive than projection. Alice has denied a part of herself that is desperate to come to the surface. She cannot flatly deny that she dislikes Bob, so instead, she projects the dislike, thinking that it is Bob who dislikes her.

This concept was anticipated by Friedrich Nietzsche: "He who fights with monsters might take care lest he thereby becomes a monster. And if you gaze for long into an abyss, the abyss gazes also into you." (Beyond Good and Evil)

When addressing psychological trauma, this defense mechanism sometimes becomes "counter projection," including an obsession to continue and remain in a recurring trauma-causing situation and a compulsive obsession with the perceived perpetrator of the trauma or its projection.

4. Rationalization

Rationalization is a defense mechanism that involves explaining an unacceptable behavior or feeling rationally or logically, avoiding the true reasons for the behavior.

For example, a person who is turned down for a date might rationalize the situation by saying they were not attracted to the other person anyway. A student might rationalize a poor exam score by blaming the instructor rather than admitting their lack of preparation.

Rationalization not only prevents anxiety, but it may also protect self-esteem and self-concept.

When trying to explain success or failure, people using this defense mechanism tend to attribute achievement to their qualities and skills while failures are blamed on other people or outside forces.

5. Regression

Regression is reverting to an earlier stage of psychological development. The concept of regression is related to the Freudian theory that personality develops through a series of stages. When a person hasn't resolved the challenges of a certain stage, they can become fixated. Regression takes you back to the stage and behaviors of that fixation.

For example, under a high level of stress, an adult might refuse to get out of bed and start their day. Instead, they might stay at home where they feel safe and secure. They might even develop vague physical complaints without any noticeable symptoms.

In childhood, these behaviors may have brought attention and comfort from a parent. To the overwhelmed adult ego, being at home and ill seems more acceptable than facing the anxiety of the day's problems.

6. Acting Out

Acting out is doing something extreme to express a feeling or thought that is creating intense anxiety. A person might act out if they don't feel able to express their feelings more acceptably. Extreme behavior relieves the intensity of the bad feeling in the short term. As with the other primitive defenses, it is ineffective as a way of managing anxiety in the long term.

For example, a person who is angry and frustrated with their circumstances at home might act out by punching a hole in a wall. They might feel unable to identify their feelings and put them into words. Punching the wall provides quick, temporary relief of anxiety despite the bruised fist.

7. Dissociation

Dissociation is psychologically removing yourself from your present experience. It isn't done consciously; therefore, it's easy to lose track of time and memories from that time. The person who dissociates is briefly disconnecting from reality. This dissociation allows the ego to ignore anxiety triggered by that reality. Dissociation often affects people who have experienced trauma such as violence or childhood abuse.

For example, there is a broad range of behavior that can be described as dissociation. On one end of the spectrum are common and mild dissociations such as daydreaming or "highway hypnosis." At the other end is dissociation in response to a trigger related to prior trauma.

An example of extreme dissociation is a person who detaches from the present when they ride as a passenger in a car after having been involved in a tragic accident. They appear detached from the present as they are trying to mentally avoid the fear and terror of the past accident. The detachment can last for minutes, hours, days, or longer.

8. Reaction Formation

Reaction formation is acting in a way that is opposite to what you are feeling or thinking. By acting oppositely, a person can hide their true feelings even from themself. It is more likely to be a defense used by those who are out of touch with their feelings or impulses.

For example, a person who applauds with enthusiasm when their competitor wins an award can be experiencing a reaction formation. They might be unable to acknowledge their disappointment or feeling of failure at the moment. By acting enthused for the winner, the anxiety associated with the threat to their self-esteem is avoided.

9. Avoidance

Avoidance is the refusal to think about or deal with people, places, or situations that cause anxiety or guilt. It is often used by those suffering from post-traumatic stress disorder (PTSD) to avoid the place where the trauma occurred.

For example, a teenager who has had the experience of being stuck in an elevator might later avoid elevators as a means of avoiding the anxiety associated with that experience. The defense can be helpful for a while, but it sometimes becomes difficult to avoid the situation. In this case, avoidance coping itself could lead to new problems such as inefficiency.

10. Compartmentalization

Compartmentalization is blocking out awareness of certain parts of your personality. It's similar to dissociation but less extreme. If you act in a way that is inconsistent with your values, you may compartmentalize that action and block it from your awareness. It can also be understood as separating parts of your life into different categories to avoid anxiety.

For example, a person might be honest in their routine management of money and then cheat on their income tax return. They don't see the discrepancy between valuing honesty with finances and being dishonest with tax filing. They have compartmentalized the behavior of paying their taxes.

11. Displacement

Displacement is the redirecting of feelings or impulses about one person toward another less-threatening person. It's often used when the person feels that it's unsafe or unwise to direct the feelings toward the actual person involved in the problem. Most commonly, feelings of aggression are displaced. As a defense mechanism, it isn't effective because it tends to cause new problems by involving other people.

For example, think of the person who gets angry at their boss but displaces that anger toward their spouse. The expression of angry feelings toward their boss is considered unacceptable, maybe due to the threat of losing the job. It feels relatively safer to get angry at their spouse, who is unlikely to set a serious consequences.

12. Intellectualization

Intellectualization is the avoidance of feelings in an emotional situation and, instead, focusing on thoughts and using logic. It is an overemphasis on thoughts to protect ourselves from the anxiety or stress of the moment. Since the feelings are blocked from awareness, they are not managed well. The person reacts to the facts and acts on them by doing what is rational or necessary.

Rather than deal with the pain associated with emotions, a person might employ intellectualization to distance themselves from the impulse, event, or behavior. For instance, a person who has just been given a terminal medical diagnosis, instead of expressing their sadness and grief, focuses instead on the details of all possible fruitless medical procedures.

For example, a person might be told that a loved one has passed away and quickly begin to make arrangements for a burial or memorial service. The intense feelings of grief are blocked from awareness and replaced with a focus on what needs to be done. This defense becomes more problematic if it continues over time and prevents the person from acknowledging their loss and working through their grief.

13. Rationalization

Rationalization is the use of logic or reasoning to justify something upsetting that occurred. The actual reasons for the event are avoided and replaced with other seemingly reasonable explanations. By rationalizing, you might change something difficult to accept into something that "isn't so bad." It's a form of self-deception that can be effective in the short term to reduce anxiety and protect self-esteem.

For example, someone who was rejected for a date might rationalize by telling themself they didn't find the other person attractive. It may be too painful for them to accept the lack of mutual attraction. By rationalizing, they avoid feelings of rejection and the threat to their self-image.

14. Passive-Aggression

Passive aggression is the indirect expression of anger to avoid directly dealing with anger. This defense mechanism is used by many adults, particularly those who are very depressed and those with personality disorders.

For example, someone who agrees to do a favor for a friend despite not wanting to might be passive-aggressive by not following through with the requested favor. As an example, they might agree to pick up a friend from the airport at a particular time and then decide to not show up. They might later make the excuse that they forgot when in fact they decided to not be there as promised.

15. Fantasy

When used as a defense mechanism, fantasy refers to retreating into your imagination to avoid stressful situations or to reach your unattainable goals. It is a defense commonly used by children, but it is also used by adults when they are feeling challenged by their circumstances.

For example, someone who has been working long hours month after month and feeling burned out might use fantasy to think about the vacation they will take when they have the opportunity. They might imagine what they do on that vacation and how they will feel.

16. Suppression

Suppression is the conscious blocking of unpleasant thoughts, impulses, or memories. A person who is suppressing is deliberately trying not to think about a disturbing thought or impulse. This is usually done to avoid feelings of anxiety or guilt. Unlike repression, suppression does not block thoughts indefinitely. They are brought back to awareness when there is an opportunity to cope with them more effectively.

For example, someone who has lied to a friend might feel guilt for doing so. They might suppress the feeling of guilt to get through their work day but decide to talk with that friend as soon as possible. Suppression is effective in letting them function at work, but it does not prevent them from dealing with the consequences of having lied.

17. Sublimation

Sublimation is channeling unacceptable thoughts or impulses into more socially acceptable behaviors. By redirecting the energy away from the unacceptable behavior and toward more healthy behavior, the person avoids causing more problems. Sublimation can be an effective way to manage aggressive or sexual impulses.

For example, someone who is feeling angry might vent their anger by doing vigorous exercise, such as working out with a punching bag. This allows for a healthy release of energy while building strength and avoiding other problems.

18. Compensation

Compensation is making up for perceived weaknesses in one area by putting more effort and focus into other aspects of your life. It is realistic to acknowledge that you cannot excel at everything and to focus on the areas where you might excel. This defense can help maintain self-confidence when faced with weaknesses.

For example, a person who shows more talent at golf than tennis might choose to spend much more of their time playing golf. When they lose a game of tennis, they might reassure themself that they're better at golf. They are accepting that they don't excel at both sports but that they are competent in at least one. This focus on their relative strengths maintains a healthy sense of confidence in their overall athletic ability.

19. Assertiveness

Assertiveness is communicating in a direct, clear, respectful way. It is stating thoughts, feelings, or needs in a way that is firm but not aggressive. It is more direct than passive communication because opinions or needs are stated clearly. However, the words used are not mean-spirited or intended as hurtful. It's a highly desirable communication skill.

Communication styles exist on a continuum, ranging from passive to aggressive, with assertiveness falling neatly in between. People who are passive and communicate passively tend to be good listeners, but rarely speak up for themselves or their own needs in a relationship. People who are aggressive and communicate aggressively tend to be good leaders, but often at the expense of being able to listen empathetically to others and their ideas and needs. People who are assertive strike a balance where they speak up for themselves, express their opinions or needs in a respectful yet firm manner, and listen when they are being spoken to. Becoming more

Assertiveness is one of the most desired communication skills and helpful defense mechanisms most people want to learn and would benefit from doing so.

For example, a person who declines to do a favor for a friend might be assertive by saying that they cannot help with that request although they do value the friendship and would like it to continue. It is not necessary to give any reasons or to make any excuses.

20. Humor

As a defense mechanism, humor is decreasing the anxiety associated with a situation by pointing out something funny or ironic about it. Humor is widely regarded as one of the higher-level defense mechanisms. Humor reduces the intensity of a situation, and places a cushion of laughter between the person and the impulses. Fantasy, when used as a defense mechanism, is the channeling of unacceptable or unattainable desires into imagination.

For example, telling a story about a funny incident from a person's life during a memorial service is an example of using humor as a defense mechanism. The laughter helps to relieve the intensity of grief at least for a few moments. It is not an avoidance of the emotion, but simply a brief relief from it.

21. Self-serving bias

This occurs when the ego needs to protect itself from criticism, both from self and from others. In self-serving bias, a person tends to exaggerate the importance of their actions or achievements. This distorts the person's reality and makes it easier for them to deal with the unpleasant feelings that result from criticism

For instance, a colleague who failed to hit their targets at work might emphasize everything they did and apportion the blame for the failure on somebody else or another external factor to avoid being criticized for the failure.

.

CHAPTER THREE
HOW DOES DEFENSE MECHANISM AFFECT OUR IDENTITY?

Did you know that identity is a mathematical term? It belongs to the scientific theory of social mathematics, which was first studied in the late 18th century by French mathematician and philosopher, Marie Jean Antoine Nicolas de Caritat, marquis de Condorcet. Identity refers to the algebraic concept of equality among citizens in terms of their legal rights and obligations.

Marquis de Condorcet, who became famous for Condorcet's paradox, came up with the term when studying the relationship between the individual and the collective as a way of formalizing the foundations of the democratic system. According to him, if a nation and/or multiple individuals "identically" accept the rules of the community, they attain the status of citizens.

However, identity has also come to express the differences between us. Simply speaking, identity is a combination of your physical and behavioral traits that define who you are. For example, your name is part of your identity, as is the form and color of your eyes and your fingerprint. This set of characteristics allows you to be definitively and uniquely recognizable.

Identity plays an important role in empowering individuals to exercise their rights and responsibilities fairly and equitably in modern society. It is imperative for social, economic, and digital inclusion as it provides access to basic human rights such as healthcare, pensions, social benefits, the ability to exercise our right to vote, and beyond. But to be able to access those rights, one needs to be able to prove that they are who they claim to be.

The process of identity development, a major task of adolescence, is often fraught with anxiety. According to theory, defense mechanisms function to control anxiety. Thus, one might expect the use of defenses to be related to identity development, as has been found. Late adolescents in the non-committed identity statuses show strong use of defenses, in contrast to those in the committed statuses (Cramer, 1995, 1998b). Further, it has been demonstrated that the use of defenses is a linear function of the degree of crisis associated with identity status (Cramer, 1997b). In the laboratory, several studies have demonstrated that experimental threat to an individual's identity results in the heightened use of defense mechanisms. This increased defense use is greater when the threatened characteristic is more central to the person's self-representation. See Cramer, 1991 a, 1998c; Grzegolowska-Klarkowska & Zolnierczyk, 1988, 1990.

Everyone experiences negative times and situations in life. It's these situations that teach us a great deal about ourselves. How will you react? Some of us can work through a situation while others rely on our defense mechanisms to make them feel better if even for a short time.

Defense mechanisms are a series of behaviors we use that attempt to separate/protect us from unpleasant events, actions, thoughts, or feelings. Sigmund Freud determined that it all boils down to protecting your ego. When you begin to feel anxious instead of just outright collapsing, your body goes into an almost fight or flight mode and begins to employ these subconscious defense mechanisms to make you feel better and eradicate bad feelings. Think of it like your ego's "get better quick pill"

Any situation that can cause uncertainty in your life triggers your mind to create a protective "shield" allowing us to cope with what is occurring. In the short term using defense mechanisms can stop us from dwelling on something for too long and allow us to move on. However, hiding behind our defense mechanisms only provides temporary relief and can do more harm than good preventing us from growing as individuals. Defense mechanisms can make you feel as though you've developed confidence when instead you've only created a false sense of comfort for yourself.

Self-Righteousness

When someone is self-righteous, he is having or shows a strong belief that his actions, opinions, etc., are right and other people's are wrong.

Self-righteous individuals are often intolerant of the opinions and behaviors of others. A self-righteous person might also be described as being uninterested in seeking an unselfish or objective standard of right and wrong, independently of how they interact with other people.

This is the identity that's attributed to him the fact that he finds every way to defend himself in times of need. He believes he's always right.

The term "self-righteous" is often considered derogatory (see, for example, journalist and essayist James Fallows' description of self-righteousness regarding Nobel Peace Prize winners) particularly because self-righteous individuals are often thought to exhibit hypocrisy due to the belief that humans are imperfect and can therefore never be infallible, an idea similar to that of the Freudian defense mechanism of reaction formation.

Pride

When it comes to our recovery, pride tells people that they have to recover alone, that they don't want anyone to know the truth about their situation, and that they shouldn't open up to anyone. People don't

Suzanne M Howard

get close to anyone who might probe too much or push them to explore themselves more deeply.

People push others away if they show too much interest or concern; don't allow anyone to make suggestions or offer advice or guidance; unable to be honest and vulnerable with other people and with themselves. We're hiding entire parts of ourselves from our consciousness and suppressing all kinds of fears, many of which we have no idea even exist. We're afraid of being judged, rejected, and shunned. We're afraid of being criticized and looked down upon. This is exactly what happens during the defense mechanism.

We're meant to connect with people, learn from them, and teach them through our experience. We're meant to share personal life stories that end up contributing to each other's roadmaps for healing. We're meant to trade informative tips and help each other prepare for the various challenges that will inevitably arise along our recovery journey. We are more likely to make meaningful changes in our lives and achieve lasting sobriety with the help of a supportive team.

However, the cause of the Defensive mechanism, all these are not feasible as we try to protect ourselves from anxiety, and the identity that portrays us is that of pride.

Distrust

Distrust is the confident expectation that another individual's motives, intentions, and behaviors are sinister and harmful to one's interests. In interdependent relationships, this often entails a sense of fear and anticipation of discomfort or danger. Distrust naturally prompts us to take steps that reduce our vulnerability in an attempt to protect our interests.

During the cause of the Defensive mechanism, individuals understand the user as being unable to accept the fact due to anxiety and therefore do not trust him. This destroys the identity and may further lead to a more harmful effect.

HOW A DEFENSE MECHANISM CAN HURT US

Oftentimes, a defense mechanism can offer instant gratification or immediate relief by alleviating our anxiety or cutting us off from a deeper level of feeling. We may not be conscious of it at the moment, but the reason we reach for that second glass of wine, pick that fight with our partner, or shy away from a challenge may be because we got scared and felt we had to retreat into our shell or put ourselves back in place.

For example, say we had an incredibly close night with our partner in which we felt both loved by them and loving toward them. That feeling can trigger myriad unconscious reactions: the anxiety of relying on that person, the fear of losing him or her, or the shame of not having felt that kind of love as a child.

The next morning, we may find ourselves feeling slightly critical and starting to act irritable. It may even feel like a relief to complain to them or make little comments that push them away. Ultimately, we no longer feel as close to the person, and although we may feel bad, we also feel a bit safer having retreated into our defense mechanism and covering over those deeper feelings being stirred.

This process of numbing our vitality and limiting our scope of connection and experience is the ultimate sacrifice we pay to our defenses. It hurts us, and it hurts those close to us. "When people are defended, they tend to neutralize their experiences and lose considerable feeling for themselves and others., "In this self-protective state, their gaze is focused inward on themselves rather than outward toward others. Their capacity for offering and accepting love is impaired, and they tend to limit personal transactions of both giving and receiving."

HOW TO BECOME THE MASTER OF YOUR DEFENSE MECHANISMS

Are you tired of your defense mechanisms undermining your happiness? You can step up to the plate for yourself and take charge, but it's going to take some concentrated action. Figure out where you're at, then weigh out the pros and cons. Figure out how these defense mechanisms are tearing you down and you can figure out how to climb out of the hole that you've dug.

1. Do a self-assessment

If someone asked you to write down your top 3 toxic defense mechanisms — what would they be? Taking more than a few seconds indicates a need to take it back to the drawing board to think things through. Until we know exactly what our issues are, there's little chance we can effectively fix them. To get yourself back to peace, you need to complete a brutally honest self-assessment.

Figure out where you're at and what defense mechanisms you're using. Pinpoint your reactions, the emotions behind those reactions, and the triggers that set off those emotions. Everything is connected. To get to the root of all your issues, you're going to have to follow the path backward and get back to a clear vantage point.

Question how you interact with others. Question who you are in times of hardship and who you are in times of elation or success. When you're feeling insecure, do you lash out? When you're feeling as though something is going "too well" do you self-sabotage and run away before you can be hurt by others? Beat your toxic self-defense tendencies by starting with some honesty.

2. Find out if it's worthwhile

Once you know the lay of the land with your defense mechanisms, you can honestly weigh out how they positively and negatively affect you. Not all defense mechanisms are created equal. Some of them bring along nasty results, while others can bring us closer together when managed delicately. Until you honestly analyze the feedback, you're getting from your behavior, though, you'll never know.

Be honest about your defense mechanisms and be honest about how you're using them (or overusing them). If they are disrupting your happiness or your life, then you need to admit it to yourself and begin thinking of ways to settle and resolve them once and for all.

Don't flinch away from the uncomfortable truths. Does your tendency to self-sabotage push away your friends, or detonate your most intimate relationships? When you deny your negative emotions, do you just make yourself feel worse in the long run? Question every inch of who you are and then think about who you want to be. If you discover more good than bad, then it's time to make some changes.

3. Tap into emotional awareness

Emotional awareness is such a powerful thing, and it can unlock a lot of doors for us in terms of self, relationships, and even our careers. When you become aware of your own emotions and how they affect you, you often also end up with a better understanding of those same emotions in others. This — in turn — helps you to relate to them, and it helps you to see things from their point of view (as well as your own).

Don't just focus on beating your defense mechanisms into the ground. Focus instead on being as mentally strong as possible, so that you are capable of managing and navigating challenges whenever they appear. Rebuild your self-confidence and be present in your body and your mind. Take notice of your emotions as they occur.

Listen to what they tell you and the paths they guide you toward. Are your emotions bringing you closer to the greater good? Or are they archaic shadows of a past you're not ready to let go of yet? The more emotionally aware we become, the more empowered we are to cut ties with the past and any relics that are eating away at our present life. Don't run from your feelings if you want to control your defense mechanisms. Embrace them.

4. Allow yourself to let go

More often than not, our defense mechanisms are leftover pieces of the past; lessons left unlearned that manifest as violent overreactions to emotionally challenging situations. Each time we encounter a situation that reminds us of a painful instance in our past, we can find ourselves reverting and regressing into old habits like putting up walls or lashing out. To let go of our defense mechanisms for good, we often have to cut ties with our past for good too.

Spend some time breaking down your defense mechanisms and make sure you pull back the cover to see where the roots are lurking. Does your tendency to deny or over-rationalize come from a childhood in which these behaviors were necessary to survive emotionally? There's often a much deeper reason that we choose to run from struggle than simple "discomfort".

Let go of those past hurts and know that you no longer have to hold on to them to be safe. Those days are gone. You can choose right now who you want to be, and you can decide what type of life you want to build for yourself. You can build happier, healthier opportunities without selling yourself short or cutting yourself off with sabotage. Reach out to a mental health professional if you're struggling. Let them guide you where you need to go.

5. Figure out who you are

Defense mechanisms are especially toxic because they can get in the way of who we are meant to be. Your defense mechanisms are a bit like an autopilot or alarm system. Taking over when we're not emotionally aware enough, or emotionally strong enough — these mechanisms handle our battles for us. Do you want to be controlled by your hard-wired responses — no matter how toxic they may be? Or do you want to become powerful enough to embrace who you want to be?

Decide right now, in this moment, who you want to be. Until you take responsibility for cultivating this person, all your little mechanisms will continue to out themselves and take over. Your weak spots are triggers that bring your worst defenses to life. Be conscious of that, but don't let it become a barrier between you and the person you want to become.

Are you tired of being the person who blows up? The person who storms off, or who denies their feelings altogether? Then you need to become a stronger, more capable version of yourself. If that's your aim, you have to start being more authentic and taking action which is authentically aligned with your values, morals, desires, and needs. When we are confident in who we are and what we're doing, there's rarely a need to go on the defensive.

LETTING GO OF A DEFENSE MECHANISM

Once we begin to catch on to our defense mechanisms and the critical inner voices that drive them, we can start to choose different actions that move us closer to a state of feeling and vitality. We can seek out the things that give our lives meaning, rather than blindly believing old messages, outdated warnings, and mean self-attacks that hold us back. For some of us, this will mean putting our phones down to connect with our children. For some, it will mean opening up to their partner, allowing them to know and love us. For some, it will mean fighting an addiction. For some, it may mean giving up control.

Whatever our defense mechanisms may be, it can bring up old feelings and anxiety to challenge them. That is why we must remember to have compassion for ourselves. It may be necessary to seek out a therapist or someone to talk to about any emotions or memories that surface as we unearth the early experiences that led us to our original defenses. However, it's valuable to remember that no matter what feelings arise, there is a huge reward in persevering and allowing ourselves to be undefended and vulnerable. While it may feel frightening at first, like sailing out upon an uncharted sea, giving up our defenses is a way of liberating ourselves and opening ourselves up to novel possibilities.

As Robert Firestone wrote:

Individuals who are less defended tend to feel freer and have a greater potential for experiencing their emotions, including an increased capacity to feel the joy and happiness of life as well as a higher tolerance for intimacy. They are also more cognizant of the pain inherent in living and appear to be more responsive and adaptive to events that impinge upon their well-being. Relatively undefended people generally feel more integrated, can live more fully and authentically, and tend to be more humane toward others.

In the short term, letting go of old defense mechanisms can feel both frightening and exciting. In the long term, we can create a new normal for ourselves that embraces the poignancy, ebbs and flows, depths, and connections that the human experience has to offer. Ultimately, we can forge our path, creating a life that has a unique meaning to us and represents who we truly are.

CHAPTER FOUR
HOW DOES DEFENSE MECHANISM AFFECT OUR EMOTIONAL AND MENTAL WELL-BEING?

Defense mechanisms are human behaviors that are used to deal with unpleasant feelings, events, thoughts, or actions. What is the first thing you do if there's a physical threat? Naturally, you do whatever you can to defend yourself. The same concept applies when there is an emotional or mental threat in your life. You use defense mechanisms to deal with them. We use such mechanisms to distance ourselves from unpleasant feelings like guilt or shame.

If you keep using defense mechanisms to avoid your feelings, they might end up wreaking havoc on your psyche. The one most crucial element which makes us who we are — humans — is our ability to experience and express a plethora of emotions.

Can you imagine yourself without the ability to feel and respond to those feelings? You would rather not, because, sans emotions, we lose a major part of our identity. Life is beautiful solely because we are gifted with the superpower to feel.

It indeed is a superpower!

Without feelings, our life would be a plain canvas or one with monochromatic colors. But a coin is always double-sided. Given a chance, you can easily recall plenty of circumstances where you have wished you lacked emotions, cursed them, and wondered why you could feel them in the first place. We have all been there.

Emotions are signals to the body about ourselves and our surroundings — when we need to protect ourselves when we need to prepare, and when we need to let go. They give us feedback about our surroundings and whether or not it is safe for us to be in. Once you shut your emotions off, you have potentially eliminated a powerful sense. Mostly, this is how our story of destruction and damage begins. We do not harm ourselves by being vulnerable or feeling things, we do so when we try to sabotage the natural process of feeling.

What do we usually do when we feel overwhelmed with emotions? Instead of letting the emotions flow, we do the worst by using all of the defense mechanisms at our disposal to ward off the feeling; anything we can get hold of — avoidance, denial, ignorance, or suppression — to take control over our emotions. What we get oblivious to is that this only leads us to be psychologically more conflicted and devastated.

Alienating our emotions as a temporary solution only brings forth graver consequences in the future. As said by Sabaa Tahir in A Torch Against The Night, "Your emotions make you human. Even the unpleasant ones have a purpose. Don't lock them away. If you ignore them, they just get louder and angrier."

1. Projection

This first common type of mental defense mechanism occurs when a person attributes their feelings of shame or insecurity to another person. This also occurs when any thoughts or feelings they may have about someone make them uncomfortable. Rather than confronting their feelings of insecurity, they may subconsciously convince themselves that the other person is the issue, not themself.

A common example of this phenomenon occurs in the schoolyard. We've all seen, in movies or real life, the school bully picking on kids for one reason or another. This bully may target another child with constant taunting and insults, but in reality, that bully is projecting his feelings of insecurity and inadequacy upon the other child. Most cases of school bullying involve projection, or one of the other common defense mechanisms, in some capacity.

2. Denial

Perhaps the most common psychological defense mechanism of them all is denial. When someone refuses to face or accept reality or facts, despite being presented with hard evidence, they are said to be in denial. This occurs when a person blocks external circumstances or events to avoid dealing with any emotional impact that they may carry.

This is commonly seen in people who are suffering from addiction or substance use issues. While a person may be fully aware of their substance use issues, they may be in denial about the negative consequences of their actions. They're avoiding reality despite the negativity of the situation being obvious to the people around them.

3. Repression

Repression occurs when a person blocks out troubling events or experiences from entering their conscious thought. Painful memories, troubling thoughts, or irrational beliefs can be upsetting. Rather than face them, a person may unconsciously choose to block them in an attempt to forget them entirely.

An example of this may include someone experiencing a traumatic event as a child, only to push that memory back into their subconscious. This memory is not gone entirely, it's simply gone from conscious thought. Think of it like putting something away in a closet. The item still exists, although it may not be directly in your line of sight.

Repressed memories can show themselves in any number of ways. They can still influence behaviors and relationships, leading to issues with trust and other things. Many people that are repressing memories aren't even aware they are doing it, that's where seeking guidance from a mental health professional can be beneficial.

4. Regression

While most commonly experienced by children, regression occurs when someone regresses to an earlier stage of maturity or development when faced with situations that cause anxiety or make a person feel threatened.

Regression as a defense mechanism is most noticeable in young children. Many children who experience traumatic events or loss may begin to act as if they're in an earlier stage of development. Some examples of regression behavior in children may include sucking their thumb or wetting the bed.

Regression in adults can be similar but also has its own set of symptoms. An adult who is having trouble coping with trauma may regress to sleeping with a childhood stuffed animal, or binge-eat foods from their childhood that make them feel comfortable. Many psychologists believe that for people suffering from substance use issues, relapsing may be a form of regression. The person is regressing to using a substance that once made them feel happy or comfortable.

5. Rationalization

One common defense mechanism occurs when a person explains negative behaviors by presenting their own set of logical reasons or explanations. This allows the person to feel comfortable with their actions or choices while realizing, on some level, that they aren't correct.

One example of this in the workplace may involve one worker lashing out at a co-worker for missing a deadline on an assignment, while completely ignoring they are frequently late on deadlines as well.

This also occurs in people who suffer from substance use disorders. For example, a person may have arbitrary rules and tell themselves "my substance use isn't an issue because I'm still able to pay all of my bills." This rationalization may completely ignore how the person is neglecting their relationships or other aspects of their life.

6. Compartmentalization

Not all mental defense mechanisms are inherently unhealthy. Compartmentalization can be an effective way to manage multiple stressors if done healthily. It involves a person separating their life into independent sectors to keep stress from one part of their life from leaking into the other parts.

It can also be unhealthy. Compartmentalization entails a person building mental walls to prevent inner conflict. This can often lead to logical contradictions in a person's personality. For example, consider a scientist who is also a deeply religious person. Because they can block off parts of their mind into cognitive compartments, they can have complete faith while at church but question the logic of everything while in the laboratory.

The most common form of this defense mechanism occurs when someone prefers to keep their work-life separate from their home life and vice versa. While at home, a person may block off, or compartmentalize, their stresses from work to avoid anxieties at home.

7. Intellectualization

Intellectualization involves focusing on the intellectual rather than the emotional consequences of a situation. This removal of all emotions allows a person to use reason and logic to avoid anxiety-inducing or uncomfortable situations.

For example, if a person's partner were to move out unexpectedly, they may respond by forming a detailed financial plan for the next six months rather than addressing how their partner leaving makes them feel. The negative emotional feelings of the breakup may manifest themselves in ways that a person doesn't even realize.

While this defense mechanism can be useful in certain situations, it can also cause people to downplay or not realize the importance of their own emotions and feelings. Rather, this person may treat all difficult situations as objective problems that must be solved.

8. Sublimation

Sublimation is another common defense mechanism that can be positive if utilized healthily. It requires a slightly more self-aware approach to be done correctly. It occurs when a person channels their socially unacceptable impulses or behaviors into socially acceptable actions and behaviors. In many cases, this can result in the long-term conversion of the initial unhealthy impulse into something more acceptable.

This type of behavior is often found in people who suffer from addiction, either substance or sexual. Many people in recovery channel their negative urges into things such as exercise and other physical activities.

One example of sublimation as a defense mechanism involves intrusive sexual urges. Consider a married man going out of town on business who experiences strong urges to have an affair and cheat on his wife. A way to sublimate these feelings would be to channel them into learning more about the city, and his industry, or expanding his network of business associates.

9. Displacement

Displacement as a defense mechanism involves redirecting an emotional reaction from the rightful recipient to another person altogether. Typically this is a child or another person that poses no threat. This allows a person to satisfy their need to react while avoiding the potentially awkward confrontation with the person they're angry with.

Someone who uses displacement as a strategy may have a difficult day at work and not deal with it appropriately. The natural reaction to being treated unfairly at work would be to address the situation with the human resources department or another higher authority. Rather than react appropriately, our subject opts to take his aggression out on his spouse and child. Neither of these people deserves to be the target of his strong negative emotions, but the consequences of taking his anger out on them are lesser than the consequences of lashing out at his boss.

10. Reaction Formation

This defense mechanism involves expressing or behaving in a manner that is the opposite of a person's true feelings. Typically, the person is fully aware of how they or feel but chooses to act in a manner that is opposite of their instincts. Think of this as denial taken to an extreme point. A person who uses reaction formation as a defense mechanism may start to show conscious behaviors to overcompensate for the anxiety they feel regarding unconscious thoughts or emotions that they deem as socially unacceptable.

A classic example of reaction formation can occur in the workplace. For instance, a woman who is very angry with her boss and would like to quit her job may instead be overly kind and generous toward her boss and express a desire to keep working there forever. She is incapable of expressing the negative emotions of anger and unhappiness with her job and instead becomes overly kind to publicly demonstrate her lack of anger and unhappiness.

How Locus Of Control And Defense Mechanisms Impair Our Mental Well-Being And Social Functioning

Many a time, we wonder why we often fail at personal development, personal branding, social relationships (family, work romantic or friendship), etc. It could be a result of unhealthy use of cognitive heuristics (Jay & Darwyn 1979) which is often an unintentional behavioral pattern. When we get to identify these behavioral patterns, we become mindful and respond in a healthier way to stress-inducing stimuli that may prompt us to resort to them (maladaptive cognitive processes) as a means of coping mechanisms. Being mindful and responding in healthy manners helps our psychological and social functioning become more optimal and our growth becomes inevitably progressive. All of the great people we admire today have at some point read about these concepts in books or learned in particular seminars, so they have learned to do away with them or simply intentionally reduce their use of them. Set of constructive behaviors build a better and happier life for us.

Below is an explanation of how our personal growth and mental health are inhibited by the unhealthy use of locus of control and defense mechanisms.

Locus of control

Locus of Control is a construct that is said to be part of our personality (Rotter, 1966). It is a continuum that runs from a strong external locus of control at one end of the continuum to a strong internal locus of control at the other end (Drew, 2018). The basic idea of locus of control is that it describes the extent an individual feels in control of what happens to them and the extent to which they, as an individual, can influence changes in their own life. For instance, their ability to alter maladaptive thought processes, decision-making, their current financial position, their grades in school, etc.

A strong external locus of control describes when someone believes what happens to them is luck or fate and that they are not in control of their life; it is all due to external forces in their environment (for example other people) (Drew, 2018).

Some people believe that whatever comes their way is majorly influenced by external factors. For example, a person who often fails exams might attribute the failure to the lecturer's sadistic attitude, and a person who faces intense financial struggle might attribute the struggle to the government or the fate determined by a Supreme power.

The latter may truly exist but to believe that such power is directly responsible for our personal choices may reduce our ability to be proactive in causing significant changes in our personal lives. A strong external locus of control usually aggravates marital, financial, and social problems. The psychological implication is that a person may develop low self-esteem because even if good things happen to them, they attribute it to external influences.

However, this may reduce overwhelming feelings of anxiety and depression because it makes people feel whatever happens is not influenced by them. With a strong external locus of control, a person who notices say, anti-social behaviors in his or her child may ignore the fact that a psychologist or mental health professional needs to be seen because usually these professionals often talk people into actions meanwhile many these people believe personal problems are caused by external factors. Therefore they may prefer to see a priest who would confirm their belief that the problems are triggered by external forces.

External locus of control as a method of perceiving the world reduces our power and ability to control the controllable situations in our lives. It renders us helpless and insecure. It causes a person to be excited easily by external influences; people who have anger problems often adopt an external locus of control.

Another instance is a business owner who only needs to gather some marketing skills to boost his or her business, and will rather focus on altering external factors perceived to be causing the hindrance, e.g, he or she may seek ways to sabotage his or her competitors or collecting some diabolical items to keep in the business arena.

A society where they suffer from socio-economic problems tends to constitute many individuals that use more of this locus of control. They take everything as it comes believing that they are only passively existing and that things they experience have nothing to do with their personal decisions, choices, perceptions, etc. This may also affect conflicts, for instance, within a family context. When something goes wrong, every person believes it's the fault of someone else; therefore, they take no responsibility for the situation.

Meanwhile, if each person takes responsibility, issues get resolved easily and progressive changes are conspicuous. A boss or colleague at work who often points fingers is demonstrating an external locus of control.

This external locus of control is logical enough to provide justifications for many problems in society attributable to an aggregate of behavioral problems.

The truth of the matter is that the more we realize we in a way influence how our lives evolve as we exist, the more control we have over situations in our lives and the more progressive our personal growth is

To live a more harmonious and successful life, a person must understand when blame is to be shared, when others need to be truly scolded and when we are meant to take the blame and ensure we play active roles in alleviating the circumstance.

A strong internal locus of control describes someone who believes they are in control of what happens to them. As an example, imagine Don does not do well in an examination, he may say that it is because he didn't work hard enough, and should have revised more, this would mean he has an internal locus of control because he sees herself as to blame for the failure. Conversely, he could say that it was because the teacher couldn't teach and the exam was not fair. This would suggest that he has an external locus of control and sees external reasons for the failure.

Internal locus of control causes a person to feel utterly feel responsible for both fair and unfair situations in their lives. This has more advantages because people who utilize this locus of control may easily be prompted to take proactive measures to improve their lives.

Another psychological implication is that it causes a person to feel overly overwhelmed by unfavorable situations so this may trigger symptoms of depression, Obsessive Compulsive Disorder (OCD), other personality disorders, etc. For instance, a person may always criticize themselves for almost everything that goes wrong in their lives.

They may give little chance for others to take responsibility for situations, this could result in interpersonal deficiency, meaning that they may avoid relationships because they believe they are not enough. They rarely get satisfied with things, they internalize every issue. This is usually toxic for mental and physical health. Also, this locus of control might reflect ostentatious behaviors in that a person may attribute their success to their efforts. They exaggerate their abilities, and this may offend others.

To stay healthy is to use both external and internal locus of control moderately. Pay attention to every situation and understand when personal factors have influenced a situation or when to internalize the issues, and when the external factors need to be altered to suit our well-being. However, it is vital to understand that our internal characteristics (attitudes, personality, etc.) have a major influence on our perceptions of and reactions to events. Therefore, for optimal functioning, we must focus on our personal growth and improve our cognition.

Defense mechanisms

In addition to explaining how our maladaptive behaviors cause life problems that impede our growth, Freud proposed several defense mechanisms that have been observed to be used by humans to alleviate anxiety triggered by conflicts between inner forces (superego that represents moral principles and id that represents impulsive drives). Inner conflicts and anxiety are not major causes of psychological disorders, but they may do so when a particular defense mechanism is relied on too heavily. Defense mechanisms are cognitive strategies frequently employed by the ego which work to transform the conflicts in a way that prevents unacceptable thoughts and feelings from reaching consciousness. If successful, defense mechanisms can immediately decrease anxiety.

For instance, someone may ascribe anxiety-inducing thoughts to others. This is known as projection, e.g, instead of admitting that you don't like to work with others, you convince yourself and others that particular persons don't like to work with others. This projection may explain misconceptions and other interpersonal problems. It causes trust issues in a relationship (e.g., romantic, work, friendship, etc.). Adopting this excessively may also lead to paranoia or anxiety disorder which have adverse effects on our well-being.

It is important to pay attention to our thoughts and ensure we confirm our assumptions by engaging in prompt communication that gives room for free sincere expressions and why another defense mechanism that is often adopted is denial. This is the failure to acknowledge the anxiety-inducing thoughts. For example, a person who exhibits intense mood swings and shows other symptoms of bipolar disorder may refuse to accept that his or her behavior is maladaptive. This would prevent insight into the problem and seeking or accepting intervention does not happen.

Understand areas of your lives you will like to improve on, you may be experiencing a problem in those areas of your life because of particular unhealthy behaviors you exhibit. Then you need to identify some of your behaviors that are not productive or healthy, then pay attention to replacing such unproductive behaviors with healthy and productive ones. For instance, if you find yourself getting overly emotional; angry, or sad, and you also don't seem to perform well socially, spiritually, and or academically. You may first need to gain insight into psychological factors such as your perception, emotional regulation, etc. When you focus on alleviating your maladaptive psychological constructs (cognitions, emotions, attitudes, etc.) your behaviors become more constructive and productive. You will then begin to experience conspicuous positive changes in your life.

CHAPTER FIVE
WHICH DEFENSE MECHANISM CAN HURT A RELATIONSHIP?

Healthy relationships are critical to a great life. There are few joys that can compare to connection with others. In addition, who you choose to associate with can make or break your entire future. But having great relationships takes more than choosing the right people for your inner circle – it takes dedication, humility, and skill from you to nurture those relationships so that they thrive. The hardest part of relationships is handling conflict, because conflict triggers your defense mechanisms.

Defense mechanisms are those negative knee-jerk reactions you have when somebody hurts you or confronts you. They're reflexes that you picked up somewhere along the way as a response to a pain that you experienced. These responses can destroy your relationship because they drive a rift between you and the other person. Defense mechanisms kick in when we're afraid, and when we're afraid, we make a mess.

As human beings, we use defense mechanisms from time to time whether we realize it or not. This is fine...until it starts getting in the way of your relationships. These mechanisms are something we use to comfort ourselves. Humans use defense mechanisms to protect themselves from all sorts of scary feelings such as heartbreak, failure, vulnerability and more

However, sometimes these defense mechanisms hurt you more than they help you. Defense mechanisms often push others away, even if that's not what you intend.

When you are in a romantic relationship, it's a good idea to evaluate defense mechanisms that you may be using. If you feel that you are subconsciously pushing your partner away, take a step back and look at your actions from an outside perspective.

If these sound familiar to you, you might be killing your relationship with your defense mechanisms.

Being able to maintain reasonable relationships is a pretty necessary ingredient for a happy and functional lifestyle, inasmuch as relationships are a primary means for satisfying basic human needs for affection, attachment and economic support. Defenses based on more accurate understandings of social reality tend to enhance people's functioning and their ability to relate to others. Vice versa, defenses based on more primitive, distorted understandings of social reality tend to sabotage people's ability to distinguish good from bad relationships. Knowing this, it may strike you as ironic to note that relationships are perhaps the best means known through which people whose representation of social reality are faulty can receive correction (Such folk need to be in healthy relationships to mature, but they all too frequently sabotage those relationships to which they have access).

How do your defense mechanisms affect your romantic relationships?

If you tend to use them in an unhealthy way, they can create distance between you and your partner, and make it difficult to connect on a deeper level. Here are some ways that your defense mechanisms might affect your relationship:

1. You might withdraw from your partner when you're feeling anxious or threatened.

If you tend to use withdrawal as a defense mechanism, you might find yourself pulling away from your partner when you're feeling stressed or overwhelmed. This can make it difficult for your partner to feel close to you, and can create distance in the relationship.

2. You might become overly dependent on your partner.

If you tend to use dependence as a defense mechanism, you might find yourself becoming overly reliant on your partner for emotional support. This can make it difficult for you to stand on your own, and can put a lot of pressure on your partner.

3. You might try to control your partner.

If you tend to use control as a defense mechanism, you might find yourself trying to control your partner in an attempt to feel safe and secure. This can be frustrating and suffocating for your partner, and can lead to conflict and tension in the relationship.

4. You might become overly critical of your partner.

If you tend to use criticism as a defense mechanism, you might find yourself being overly critical of your partner. This can make it difficult for your partner to feel good about themselves, and can damage the self-esteem.

5. You might shut down emotionally.

If you tend to use emotional shutdown as a defense mechanism, you might find yourself shutting down emotionally in your relationship. This can make it difficult for your partner to connect with you on a deeper level, and can lead to feelings of loneliness and isolation.

DEFENSE MECHANISMS THAT CAN HURT RELATIONSHIPS

When they go out of hand, defense mechanisms can keep you "safe" in your bubble, preventing you from facing emotional problems and advancing in your emotional life. Unfortunately, repressed emotions and feelings can show up and impact your wellbeing in all kinds of unpleasant ways.

For example, you may find it difficult to open up to potential partners or withdraw from your existing partner. You may also idealize your partner and get sorely disappointed when they don't turn out to match your fantasy. You can be in denial of negative occurrences and behaviors, letting them harm you indefinitely and making it harder to break away from unhealthy relationship dynamics. The list goes on.

Your unconscious defense mechanisms can damage your romantic relationships in many ways, especially if you remain unaware of them. This is why it's a good idea to learn about common survival strategies and see which ones may apply to you.

1. Projection

Projection may damage intimate relationships, often requiring partners to visit private couple retreats for reconnection. Projection may work differently for each person. Nevertheless, there are some general examples you may have come across in your life:

- A cheating partner suspects that the other person in the relationship is being unfaithful. They project their own infidelity to their partner, transferring their own behaviors and shame.

- You interrupt a person who talks too much and they accuse you of being a poor listener or conversationalist.

- You strongly dislike someone and convince yourself that they are the one who doesn't like you.

- You are able to complete a task successfully and believe that everyone else can do it, too.

As you can probably tell, projection can manifest itself in an endless variety of ways. Essentially, it involves instances where people accuse others of their own, often maladaptive tendencies and behaviors.

What Is Projection In A Relationship?

Projection most commonly occurs in romantic relationships, where each partner may, in a way, borrow their partner's identity or attribute their own traits to them. Unfortunately, it is quite common for people to project everything they don't like about themselves onto their partner. This can prevent the relationship from progressing, as well as stump your own psychological growth.

One unfortunate effect of projection is that it may make you feel like a victim of life. You may feel like everything bad that happens to you is your partner's fault. Or your parents may be to blame. This can encourage you to repeat maladaptive behaviors and damage your relationship

Furthermore, it may impede your self-development and your capability for building a genuine connection with your partner. Displacing your negative thoughts and emotions which can sometimes do irreparable damage to your relationship, especially if you don't make an effort to detect your own projections.

What Causes Psychological Projection?

Like many other defense mechanisms such as reaction formation and the repression of unwanted memories, projection boils down to self-defense. You may project because you are unable to acknowledge a negative quality or painful thoughts. It is often easier to displace difficult emotions to others, than it is to take responsibility for your actions and confront the aspects of your personality you don't like.

By projecting, you try to keep pain, shame, and guilt at bay. It is also more comfortable for people to see negative qualities in other people than in themselves. The people who are prone to projecting often don't understand themselves very well, even if they believe that they do. Low self-esteem and feelings of inferiority may also cause you to project your negative thoughts and behaviors onto others.

If you are struggling to spot symptoms of projection in yourself and still feel as if your partner or a friend gets under your skin too much, you can try asking yourself the following questions:

- What experience from my past is triggered by this experience?

- What do I feel when speaking with or thinking about this person?

- What am I saying and thinking about this person?

- Am I reactive in the situation and why?

- What does this remind me of? Is it another situation or a person?

- How am I like this person? In what ways am I different?

- Is it possible that other people see me this way, too? Why do I fear that?

- What can I do to feel better?

- Can I set healthy boundaries with this situation or person?

- How can I be more compassionate?

2. Stonewalling

No relationship is without conflict. Even the healthiest relationships will have some friction from time to time. While it's natural not to see eye-to-eye with your partner, it's how you handle those disagreements that can determine whether it helps or harms your relationship.

When you and your partner are faced with a conflict, do you calmly hash it out or does one partner stonewall, or give the silent treatment?

While stonewalling may seem like a harmless tactic to deal with problems in your relationship, it can have disastrous effects and may even be a pathway to divorce. However, there is hope for both parties.

We dive into what stonewalling is, the signs to look out for and how to break down this wall that's dividing your relationship.

What does it mean to stonewall someone?

In simple terms, stonewalling is when someone completely shuts down in a conversation or refuses to interact with another person.

"It is a voluntary response aimed at ending a conversation or a situation that triggers emotional unrest or discomfort, resulting in an overwhelming physiologic response,

This is a state where the person stonewalling is either confused or shocked by a conversation or a set of questions."

Oftentimes, stonewalling is quite noticeable in relationships. However, there are times when stonewalling may go unnoticed—especially if neither partner is aware of their behaviors.

How can I tell if I'm being stonewalled by my partner?

A person can stonewall in several different ways. If you aren't sure if your partner is stonewalling you or not, here are some of the following signs to look out for:

- They walk out in the middle of a conversation without warning or explanation

- They refuse to talk about or give reasons not to talk about an issue

- They dismiss your concerns

- They engage in passive-aggressive type behavior

- They change the subject or make accusations to avoid an issue

- They give you the silent treatment, avoiding nonverbal communication such as making eye contact with you

What if I am stonewalling my partner?

When you're on the receiving end of stonewalling, it may be more obvious to notice the effects their behavior has on you. But what if you're the one refusing to cooperate? Here's how to tell if you tend to stonewall:

- You avoid conflicts and arguments in any possible way

- You get very defensive when your partner addresses a concern

- You hide your true feelings and opinions

- You have a hard time admitting when you're wrong

What are the negative effects of stonewalling on relationships?

The effects of stonewalling are disastrous for not only the receiver but also the partner who's stonewalling.

For the person being stonewalled, it can leave them feeling confused, hurt and angry. It can wear down on their self-esteem, leading them to feel worthless or hopeless.

For the person stonewalling, they also suffer as they are denying themselves emotional intimacy with their partner.

For the couple, stonewalling can build a giant divide in their relationship, causing severe marital distress, conflict and disruption.

How do you deal with stonewalling in your relationship?

If stonewalling is occurring in your relationship, the best thing to do is to face it head-on as a couple and not bury your heads in the sand. To make your relationship work, you need to work together. To do this, you'll both need to learn how to communicate more effectively. This situation is one where couples counseling can help.

"Whether you or your loved one is stonewalling, if frequent episodes lead to escalated misunderstandings and miscommunication that affects trust in your relationship, then professional help can help assess and address those communication issues

Getting couples counseling can help you learn healthy ways to communicate and may help to strengthen your relationship as a whole.

3. Displacement

Have you ever taken your work frustrations out on your partner? If so, then you exhibited displacement. Displacement is the act of redirecting negative emotions and thoughts from their source and acting them out on a less threatening subject.

People who work toxic, stressful, or just frustrating jobs are usually not in a position to work out the issues with their boss. Perhaps their boss is not understanding or is too imposing to approach. Therefore, many people use displacement as a way to deal with their emotions. They come home angry with work but take it out on their partners and children, who are less likely to be a threat.

Obviously, this can quickly hurt a relationship. In many cases, the victim of displacement has not done anything to deserve such a reaction. This can leave them hurt and confused. Those who use displacement may find minor issues to use to take out their anger on, wearing down their partner and pushing them away.

4. Regression

Have you experienced backward movement in your personality or in the personality of someone you love? Perhaps a situation pushed you to behave as though you were living ten years prior, or your significant other has started acting incredibly childish. If so, you may be experiencing or witnessing regression.

To regress is to go backward. Do you ever feel like you exhibit immature childlike behavior when you are under a tremendous amount of stress? You may be displaying the defense mechanism of regression. If you are under stress, whether it relates to your relationship or not, you might notice yourself acting clingy. For example, you might get really upset when your partner leaves you for just a night or two.

If you act like it's the end of the world when your partner goes out of town for the weekend, you will likely end up pushing them away. This type of behavior is not cute when it goes on for too long and will end up sabotaging your relationship.

How Regression Applies To Your Relationship

It can be confusing for those in a relationship to experience regression firsthand or witness it in a significant other. Imagine your loved one suddenly acting out or as though they were a child. This can cause some complications in a relationship. When your partner is suddenly throwing temper tantrums that are uncharacteristic of them, has picked up a former bad habit, or is wetting the bed, the relationship can face more challenges than it was prepared for.

Experiencing such drastic changes in a relationship can feel as though your significant other is no longer themselves. It is often difficult to remain in a relationship when the person you know is no longer acting like the person you love and care for. If regression is altering your relationship, couples counseling might be a way for you to work on your relationship, yourself, and your loved one's regression. It may be necessary for the individual experiencing a regression also to have solo therapy sessions.

Therapy is a common and helpful tool in treating several relationships and individual problems and concerns. Seeking help is the best way to make it through psychological challenges in the best headspace. While there is no magic cure for these kinds of issues, putting in the effort and work to stay together or to be better is key.

Three Issues That Intensify Regression

First, a partner may hold a powerful inhibition against wanting something that they do desire in the relationship. The more unable they are to be direct about the desire, the more this spouse will exhibit their desire through regressed behavior. An extreme example of this occurred with a wife who wanted to be a stay-at-home mom. Unable to negotiate or problem-solve about this directly with her husband, she became increasingly depressed and non-functional at work until she was put on disability leave and forced to stay at home.

Secondly, some partners have a powerful inhibition against even knowing what they want and desire. This results in their easily emerging with a partner, not activating their own thinking and becoming highly dependent on the spouse.

Last, some partners feel wrong for expressing their desires and feel powerful guilt when they do express them. They may have come from homes where having personal desires was defined as selfish or greedy. These partners tend to regress in couples' sessions and hope that the other "will read my mind." They also frequently withdraw from their sexual relationships rather than risking putting their desires into words. The inhibition of their desires and non-action protects them from feeling the shame or guilt of being wrong or bad.

In all of the above issues, direct knowledge or expression of internal desires puts the client into an internal conflict. The conflict exists between the want or desire and the internalized, intrapsychic parent who says it is not ok to want or desire.

As a result, regression to earlier coping mechanisms occurs when a spouse fears being direct or when they can not allow themselves to want directly. Regression also occurs when a spouse distorts the behavior of their partner, and the behavior becomes a transference trigger. Partners who don't have the capacity or skill to check out their perceptions will move deeper into a transferentially-triggered regression. Other partners hold tightly to regressive/symbiotic beliefs like, "A relationship should be easy. I shouldn't have to work this hard. I shouldn't have to put my desires into words."

How the Therapist May Inadvertently Contribute to Increasing Regression

Couples therapists may inadvertently support or induce regression during a couples' session. Have you ever asked a partner to tell their spouse what they want? And after they have done what you asked, did you end up with a pit in your stomach, recognizing that you were now in a mess? Maybe Joe has asked Ann to love him for who he is. He has done what you asked. But you know his request is impossible. You know Ann can't deliver. Now you must either correct him, which places you in a difficult parental role, or support an infantile regressed and impossible desire. Neither alternative is very good.

In a couple's session, don't say, "Ask for what you want." This sets up a regressed orientation in which one partner goes to the other as if on bended knee. This partner is then at the mercy of the other's good will. It is much more effective to say instead, "Describe your desires to your partner, and tell him (or her) what it would mean to you to be able to realize your desires. Then I will also ask you to listen to what your partner desires."

A therapist may also be overly supportive of a regressed partner. Perhaps you find the client's rage intimidating. Perhaps their pain resonates with some pain or loss that you have experienced. Perhaps the client does not want to self-activate in an arena that you also find difficult. A common example is women not wanting to think about money and finances.

You may end up being overly nurturing, too helpful, or especially empathic, without leading them out of or confronting the regression. This process may be especially intense when you get attacked for not being caring or sympathetic. You may feel anxious, desire to avoid the attack, and end up being too nice or overly giving. Sadly, this will not help the client master their regression. An alternative is to listen actively, acknowledge the distress, empathize and then even say, "It feels good to be understood." After that it is time to work actively on a way out of the regression.

5. Altruism

This defense mechanism is a bit different from the others because it doesn't feature outright negative behavior like the rest. When you engage in altruistic behavior you use kindness towards others to defuse an anxious situation.

If you feel that your partner is upset with you, you might start overcompensating with niceness. This type of defense mechanism will kill a relationship in a different way than the rest.

When you are overly nice to your partner every time you want to turn around a negative situation, your partner will begin to notice. This may lead to your partner taking advantage of you and treating you unfairly.

In the case that you feel there is a problem in your relationship, it's always better, to be honest, and talk about it with your partner, rather than trying to resolve it the least confrontational way possible.

6. Denial

Denial is perhaps the most commonly known defense mechanism. When someone is in denial, they are rejecting the current reality in front of them because it makes them uncomfortable. Instead of accepting the situation, they act as though it does not exist. This is a way to avoid the situation altogether, because it is too distressing to acknowledge its existence.

This can be quite damaging in relationships. Those who use denial as a defense mechanism often deny that they do or say anything that hurts their loved ones. When confronted, the person in denial will act as though the things they did and said never happened. Depending on how conscious the person is of their actions, this could potentially lead to gaslighting.

Ignoring reality does not make it go away. Denial only pushes the situation farther down the road, often leading to bigger and more damaging problems. This defense also deteriorates relationships quickly as loved ones learn not to discuss their needs or any issues that they have.

Have you ever tried to discuss your defense mechanisms with a partner before? How did it go?

If you're like most people, it probably didn't go as smoothly as you would have hoped.

One of the biggest challenges in any relationship is communicating effectively about difficult topics – and our defense mechanisms are often a big part of that. We all have them, but we don't always know how to talk about them in a way that our partner will understand.

If you're not sure how to start the conversation, here are a few tips:

1. Be honest about your feelings

The first step is to be honest with yourself about how you're feeling. What are you afraid of? What are you trying to protect yourself from? Once you have a better understanding of your own feelings, you'll be in a better position to explain them to your partner.

2. Choose the right time to talk

Try to pick a time when both of you are relaxed and don't have anything else on your mind. It's also important to be respectful of your partner's feelings – if they're not in the mood to talk about this right now, don't force the issue.

3. Be open to hearing your partner's perspective

Your partner may have their own defense mechanisms that you're not aware of. It's important to be open to hearing their side of the story and understanding where they're coming from.

4. Avoid blaming or judgment

If you want your partner to be open to hearing what you have to say, it's important to avoid blaming or judging them. This will only make them defensive and less likely to listen to you.

5. Focus on the future

Try to focus on how you can work together to overcome your defense mechanisms and build a stronger relationship. This is a team effort, and it's important to approach it with that mindset.

Final Thoughts

Did you identify with any of these defense mechanisms? Have you begun to realize how they can negatively affect your relationships?

Having this awareness is the key to improving. If you identify with any of these behaviors, the good news is that you can develop healthier coping strategies. By using mindfulness, inner work, and working with a therapist, you can develop more mature defense mechanisms that are not harmful to your relationships.

CHAPTER SIX
COPING WITH UNHEALTHY DEFENSE MECHANISM

In psychoanalytic theory, a person's experience of the "self" is referred to as the ego. The ego has certain boundaries in terms of what is considered to be or not to be a part of oneself or one's identity. As personality solidifies through life experience, a person develops emotional triggers where certain kinds of thoughts, feelings, impulses, people, objects, or events are perceived as undesirable or unacceptable because they threaten the boundaries of the ego.

When this happens, a person will unconsciously engage in self-defense or self-protection. Sigmund Freud pioneered the study of defense mechanisms to explain the many strategies that people use to cope when reality unfolds contrary to expectations.

Defense mechanisms are attempts to counter psychological stress or negative emotions and, since they are usually deployed unconsciously and habitually, it is difficult to know exactly when and why they are being activated. They are sometimes necessary when encountering highly stressful, emotionally traumatic, or emergencies but, under normal circumstances, long-term reliance on them can ruin your ability to adapt well in life because they distance you from crucial self-knowledge, eventually fragmenting the self. Therefore, the high cost of using a defense mechanism is a corresponding decrease in self-awareness and emotional intelligence.

Generally speaking, the lower a person's level of ego development, the more unconsciously and automatically they use defense mechanisms.

Learning about defense mechanisms allows you to:

- become more aware of when you are using them inappropriately in terms of producing more harm than good.

- exercise greater will and flexibility in choosing the coping strategy that is most appropriate for the situation at hand

- gradually dismantle your system of defense mechanisms when it interferes with achieving your goals, having healthy relationships, or pursuing self-improvement.

Examine, as honestly as you can, any past instances in which you used a defense mechanism to poor effect, look for habitual or long-running patterns. Get some idea about the kinds of people, events, or situations that easily trigger you to activate a defense mechanism and reflect on whether there is a way for you to stop using it when it prevents you from living life smoothly and successfully.

Since defense mechanisms are generally activated by negative emotions (especially fear, shame, guilt, and anger), it is advisable to work on improving your emotional intelligence so that you can deal with emotions directly instead of defending against them. It is also a good idea to listen to the feedback that you get from other people about any negative, defensive, or dysfunctional behavior.

Unhealthy defense mechanisms are often used to rewrite reality in one's mind or find other ways to avoid or skirt around the issue. These mechanisms often create more harm than good, damaging relationships, worsening one's mental health, or even making the issue much worse than it initially was.

Defense mechanisms are labeled as unhealthy when they produce dysfunctional behaviors that lead to negative, harmful, or destructive consequences. By contrast, healthier defense mechanisms are considered less harmful because they tend to be employed more consciously and maturely, and they can sometimes produce positive consequences if used appropriately. While anyone can theoretically use any coping strategy they want depending on the situation, there is some correlation between personality type and patterns of defense mechanisms

We all have our ways of dealing with stressful situations. Depending on our upbringing and past experiences, we may have healthy and effective mechanisms or use strategies that cause more harm than good. However, it's not always easy to identify these unhealthy defense mechanisms, as they are often unconscious behaviors.

The problem is that unhealthy defense mechanisms can cause unnecessary tension and rifts within the family. If either a parent or child consistently uses them, the family will struggle to work through conflict or overcome challenges together. This is why it is so important to identify unhealthy defense mechanisms early and treat them.

Signs of an Unhealthy Use of Defense Mechanisms

Here are seven signs of unhealthy defensiveness:

- You're often accusing others of doing things that you'd like to be doing but can't admit to, leading to relationship conflicts (projection)

- You have difficulty paying attention in stressful situations due to maladaptive daydreaming (dissociation)

- You're avoiding people, places, or things that upset you (avoidance)

- You tend to feel distrustful in relationships with no basis to be concerned (repression)

- Your friends point out that you act childishly at inappropriate times (regression)

- You often get angry or irritable with family after a difficult work day (displacement)

- You're arriving late to work routinely after using alcohol or other substances on the prior day, but you're telling yourself that you still get the work done and do not have a problem (denial).

Common Unhealthy Defense Mechanisms

i. Acting Out:

Manifesting extreme and/or dysfunctional behaviors, usually because of not being able to utilize normal means to process feelings of frustration, anger, dissatisfaction, sadness, or unhappiness. Unhealthy because pent-up emotions unconsciously drive aggressive, destructive, or violent action. Common in individuals at low levels of ego development.

ii. Avoidance:

Trying to avoid or escape from situations that cause anxiety or stress, often because of perceiving oneself as incapable of confronting a problem directly. Unhealthy because problems are left to fester, multiply, or worsen over time, lowering self-esteem to the point of helplessness or hopelessness.

iii. Compartmentalizing:

Creating a strict division of one's sense of self into separate parts to decrease full awareness and responsibility for one's actions (e.g. strictly separating private life from public persona). Unhealthy when believing that the different roles that one occupies can be used to justify inconsistent, immoral, or hypocritical behavior.

iv. Compensation:

Trying to counterbalance one's perceived weaknesses to prop up self-esteem and avoid confronting the negative aspects of oneself, usually by overemphasizing one's strengths or relying on actions that can superficially camouflage flaws/mistakes. Unhealthy because a person cannot confront their weaknesses and shortcomings, thus becoming incapable of real improvement. Common in individuals who are prone to looping or grip patterns.

v. Denial:

Conscious or unconscious refusal to accept factual reality to avoid confronting painful feelings or negative emotions. Unhealthy because a person becomes incapable of seeing and solving their problems properly, leading to negative consequences or a snowball effect. Common in individuals at low levels of ego development.

vi. Displacement:

Redirecting negative thoughts, feelings, or impulses from the source of frustration onto someone/something that is considered "inferior" or "safer" to act upon without garnering severe consequences. Unhealthy because it makes a person more prone to being abusive or exploitative. Common in individuals at low levels of ego development.

vii. Dissociation:

Disconnecting from awareness of a negative event in progress, often resulting in a person losing track of themselves, the passing of time, or awareness of physical surroundings. Unhealthy when a person cannot heal their fractured sense of self upon returning to more normal circumstances. Common in individuals who have suffered severe abuse, intense trauma, or extreme shock.

viii.Fantasy:

Using imagination to escape from reality when life is not unfolding according to one's desires, usually by exploring alternative yet unrealistic realities or engaging in wishful thinking, thereby avoiding feelings of failure, grief, or disappointment. Unhealthy when fantasy is used in place of taking effective action to improve oneself or life conditions, thus getting stuck in a rut.

ix. Idealization:

Creating a perfect ideal to focus on the positive aspects of a situation and avoid confronting the negative aspects. There is a negative form of idealization in which a person evaluates the world in terms of how things fail to measure up to imagined perfection, thus producing a mindset dominated by cynicism and/or perfectionism. Unhealthy because a person (repeatedly) sets themselves up for disappointment through unrealistic expectations, eventually becoming rigid, delusional, and/or emotionally fragile.

x. Identification:

Identifying with or mirroring the characteristics of people who are perceived as threatening, often as a means of gaining social acceptance or avoiding social punishment. Unhealthy when one avoids taking responsibility for perpetuating abusive, manipulative, exploitative, aggressive, or violent behavior.

xi. Intellectualization:

Overemphasizing thinking/reason/logic to deny the human or emotional context of a situation, usually as a means to distance oneself from undesirable feelings, emotions, impulses, stress, or threats. Unhealthy because emotions are repressed and then drive behavior unconsciously, or because "pure logic" can lead to a lack of empathy or insensitivity to suffering.

xii. Social Comparison:

Comparing oneself downward to someone who is perceived as "worse off" or associating oneself upward with someone who is perceived as "better off" to artificially bolster self-esteem. Unhealthy because it leads to a weak sense of self and prevents a person from developing genuine self-confidence and a realistic self-image

xiii. Undoing:

Feeling strongly compelled to make up for unacceptable or hurtful behaviors that were done unconsciously, usually by counteracting the damage that was done in hopes that the "wrong" will be "righted" (e.g. being extra nice to someone you snapped at but to the point of seeming fake). Unhealthy because the intention behind the behaviors is self-centered and does not adequately account for the well-being of the other person. Common in individuals at low levels of ego development who cannot properly admit to or apologize for mistakes (often due to excessive pride).

Coping with an unhealthy defense mechanism

Unhealthy reliance on defense mechanisms is often consistent with treatment for anxiety disorders. It might involve various forms of individual therapy, anger management, grief counseling, medication, or lifestyle changes.

Even though defense mechanisms are unconscious, you can indeed transform unhealthy defense mechanisms into ones that are more sustainable or healthy. The following techniques could help:

i. Become self-aware

The first step in coping with unhealthy defense mechanisms is accepting that you use them in the first place. Once you're able to recognize when you're using them, you can dig deeper to identify your emotions. Once you identify them, you can easily start with the transformation you need.

ii. Therapy

Several forms of therapy could help limit the use of defense mechanisms. Anger management is typically recommended for acting out and displacement. If denial is resulting in persistent abuse of a substance, the person is likely to benefit from information and support from a recovery program. Someone repressing grief may need grief counseling, while a person with severe dissociation may need PTSD treatment.

A licensed mental health provider will be able to assess the underlying problem and make treatment recommendations. Medication could be recommended if the level of anxiety or irritability is extreme. The most common medications for anxiety issues are benzodiazepines, beta-blockers, and antidepressants, all of which would be prescribed by a licensed medical professional.

iii. Learn effective coping skills

If you have an unhealthy defense mechanism, learning new coping skills can help you better deal with uncomfortable emotions. Coping skills include meditation, establishing healthy boundaries, and asking for support.

iv.Lifestyle Changes

Lifestyle changes that have been demonstrated to help with defense mechanisms include regular exercise (to balance neurochemicals and lower levels of stress hormones), consistent and adequate sleep (to maintain both physical and mental well-being), and limited use of stimulants such as caffeine. Other lifestyle changes include implementing a mindfulness practice, spending time with supportive friends and family, and practicing self-compassion.

v. Talk To Someone

If you find that your defense mechanisms are hurting your life, it might be helpful for you to talk about the subject with somebody else. The next time somebody close to you calls you out on something or confronts you about how your behavior is affecting them, try being honest with them rather than getting defensive. A good thing to do would be to identify your defense mechanism and explain why it's beneficial for you in this situation. As long as the other person has opened up with you about their feelings, it should not be hard for you to do likewise.

vi. Having An Open Relationship With Others

When it comes down to it, the best way to deal with your defenses is open and honest communication with people who are close to you. This reduces stress by letting out feelings that might otherwise build up inside you without getting any release whatsoever. When somebody close tells you what's going on inside their head, don't be afraid to do likewise! You'll find that being open and honest can strengthen relationships rather than tear them apart.

I think that the best defense mechanism is to be open and honest with people. I think that if you can share what's going on inside of your head with somebody, you're less likely to subject yourself to unhealthy amounts of stress to keep it bottled up. It may be helpful for you to tell yourself that you are allowed to use defense mechanisms at times, but not all the time. Just remember that there is nothing wrong with using them every once in a while, but when they become a habit rather than just a means of coping then it might be time for some self-reflection so as not to let them get the best of you!

vii. Take responsibility

Start taking responsibility for your actions instead of pushing them on others. You must accept that you cannot control the way others act but you can control the way that you react.

viii. Break the patterns

Once you take responsibility, you are ready to break unhealthy defense patterns. Strategies like mindfulness, journaling, and practicing gratitude can help you shift your mindset and see the world more positively.

ix. Add Humour to life

As said by Mark Twain "The human race has one effective weapon, and that is laughter", this stands true in many ways. Using humor as a defense mechanism can play a magical role in dealing with stressful situations. When we can laugh about the embarrassing things we've done in the past, we take the shame out of the memory and replace it with a good measure of humor. This can de-stress the experience and the memory of it.

CHAPTER SEVEN
NARCISSISM AS A DEFENSE MECHANISM

Narcissism is not a disorder. It's a trait. Like a symptom. When someone has a pathological degree of narcissism - meaning an extreme, inflexible amount, then they may be diagnosed with Narcissistic Personality Disorder. Or they may not. Someone can have an extreme and inflexible degree of narcissism but not meet the specific criteria for NPD. Or they may but it may not be recognized.

This does not mean we cannot call them a narcissist. NPD is not the only disorder or problem that has elements of narcissism. There are others, and they are not all personality disorders. Even still, contrary to popular belief, a person does not have to be diagnosed with NPD or ANY disorder to be considered a narcissist. And just because they do not mean they are not narcissistic. "Narcissist" is not a diagnosis, and it doesn't need to be. It's a word we use to describe a type of person.

So if narcissism is not a disorder, why is it so problematic? Narcissism evolves as a defense mechanism against abuse or neglect most of the time. Let's say there is a child whose parent ignores them most of the time. When the child does try to get attention, the child is spoken to harshly and pushed away. As the child grows, they become a scapegoat for the parents.

The child is blamed, abused, and neglected. The parent says and does horrible things to the child. "You were a mistake, I wish you were never born, I hate you, you're worthless, you're stupid, you're ugly..." To a child, this is like hearing these things from God. Small children who are not valued by their parents do not value themselves. It would be as if God Himself came down from Heaven and told you that you were worth nothing.

The child's brain is immature and unable to defend against these words and these feelings. The only thing it can do is deny them and create a different reality for itself, so that's what it does. This is where the delusional beliefs narcissists hold come from, as well as the false self they create. The false self is the narcissist's defense against these hurtful words and the resulting hateful feelings they have for themselves. It is the wall they hide behind, the only real defense they have. It is their way of saying, "Look! I'm not bad, I'm good. I'm not worthless, I'm important. I'm not unwanted, I am necessary" and most importantly, "I'm not weak, I'm strong."

This is why it's so important to the narcissist that other people to believe in this false self. It isn't for them. It's for the narcissist. How can something be untrue if other people believe it? Narcissist has no internal regulation system for their self-worth. Without input from others, it is zero. This is what the so-called "narcissistic supply" is for. This is why they need it. Because of the abuse they suffered, they did not develop the way they were supposed to. Their mind was too preoccupied with simple survival and as a result, their emotional capabilities are stuck in toddler survival mode. They've never matured or been able to move on. They've never learned to deal with loss, control their emotions, handle frustration, or how to soothe themselves.

The narcissist, are still in an abusive situation, under attack all the time. And in a way, they are. Their mind has never resolved the feelings of shame, self-hatred, and worthlessness from when they were very young. They still experience these feelings as if the abuse is going on right now, and the abuse they heard still plays over and over in their minds.

So now instead of coming from outside, the abuse is coming from inside and has become a constant part of their inner dialogue. This is why they overreact to minor things or misperceive things as intentionally offensive or hurtful. They aren't reacting to what is happening. They are reacting to that constant internal abuse and self-hatred.

Narcissists believe they are defective, disgusting, unlovable, wretched... If your parents don't love you, you must be despicable indeed. This is how narcissists grow up. A lot of people say that the narcissists they know were not abused, they were spoiled and coddled. Indulgence is abuse too. That's why it's called "spoiling." When something is spoiled, it's ruined. Indulging - commonly called "spoiling" - a child ruins the child's potential as a person.

When a child is coddled, indulged, protected, and given everything they want, a lot of the same things happen that happen to children abused in more recognized ways. The child's development does not proceed as it should. They never learn how to handle their emotions, self-soothe, and deal with loss or disappointment and they learn to connect their worth to the actions of others. It is the same mindset: "If people don't give me what I want, it's because I am worth nothing."

Narcissism is not cruelty or being mean. Narcissism isn't not sharing things. Narcissism is self-centeredness arising from the failure to distinguish the self from external objects. This means that narcissists are unable to tell the difference between other people's feelings and their own or to regulate their internal emotionality instead of relying on others to do it for them. It is the result of arrested development, and indulgence can cause it just as much as other forms of abuse.

Imagine your self-worth truly relying on other people, to the point that if they did not do what you wanted, you didn't feel life was worth living. Imagine having to pretend you are someone else every second of every day, and being so afraid that people would find out you were a disgusting thing not worthy of love. Imagine being unable to provide for your own even basic emotional needs and simply having to suffer until someone did it for you. Imagine being unable to see that this is the problem, and instead believing that everyone in your life tortures you and wants you to suffer because they are cruel, abusive, and hate you.

This is why they react the way they do when they don't get what they want. It doesn't matter why they didn't get it in reality. It is perceived as malicious and purposeful withholding, which causes a narcissistic injury.

A narcissistic injury is something that's a threat or offense to their fragile self-worth. We could call it a "blow to the ego" and it is, but because of the way narcissists are wired, this phrase does not describe how severe of an injury it is. Narcissists interpret it as life-threatening. This is why narcissistic injuries cause narcissistic rage. They feel that they are fighting in defense of their very lives.

In a way, narcissism is the perfect defense mechanism. There is an excuse for everything, a reason why everything is someone else's fault. They never have to listen to criticism, take responsibility or blame. They have justifications for everything they do wrong. With narcissistic projection, they can project their painful or uncomfortable emotions and thoughts about themselves onto other people, and then the narcissist does not even have to own these. Everything belongs to someone else.

However, because narcissist is not truly able to separate themselves from the external world, it still all belongs to them. This is endlessly frustrating, like trying to throw a boomerang away. It just keeps coming back. It's sadly ironic that, for all their complicated and convoluted machinations designed to defend themselves against all of the abuse they believe they are experiencing, they aren't escaping anything.

They cannot escape the abuse because even though they don't realize it, it's coming from inside of them. They are only providing themselves temporary relief at best, and it comes at the expense of the very thing they need most: validation from other people. The more they blame, abuse, and hurt other people, the worse other people's opinions of them become. Eventually, these people leave, tired of the abuse and the games. Then the narcissist is left alone with the very person they hate the most: themselves.

The dynamics of narcissism

i. Primitive defense mechanisms

Narcissism is a defense mechanism related to the splitting defense mechanism. The Narcissist fails to regard other people, situations, or entities (political parties, countries, races, his workplace) as a compound of good and bad elements. He either idealizes his object - or devalues it. The object is either all good or all bad. The bad attributes are always projected, displaced, or otherwise externalized. The good ones are internalized to support the inflated (grandiose) self-concepts of the narcissist and his grandiose fantasies - and to avoid the pain of deflation and disillusionment.

The narcissist pursues narcissistic supply (attention, both positive and negative) and uses it to regulate his fragile and fluctuating sense of self-worth.

ii. The dysfunctional family

Research shows that most narcissists are born into dysfunctional families. Such families are characterized by massive denials, both internal ("you do not have a real problem, you are only pretending") and external ("you must never tell the secrets of the family to anyone"). Abuse in all forms is not uncommon in such families. These families may encourage excellence, but only as means to a narcissistic end. The parents are usually needy, emotionally immature, and narcissistic and thus unable to recognize or respect the child's emerging boundaries and emotional needs. This often leads to defective or partial socialization and problems with sexual identity.

iii. The issue of separation and individuation

According to psychodynamic theories of personal development, parents (primary objects) and, more specifically, mothers are the first agents of socialization. It is through his mother that the child explores the most important questions, the answers to which will shape his entire life. Later on, she is the subject of his nascent sexual cravings (if the child is a male) - a diffuse sense of wanting to merge, physically, as well as spiritually. This object of love is idealized and internalized and becomes part of our conscience (the superego in the psychoanalytic model).

Growing up entails the gradual detachment from the mother and the redirection of the sexual attraction from her to other, socially appropriate objects. These are the keys to an independent exploration of the world, personal autonomy, and a strong sense of self. If any of these phases is thwarted (sometimes by the mother herself, who won't "let go") the process of differentiation or separation-individuation is not completed, autonomy and a coherent sense of self are not achieved and the person is characterized by dependence and immaturity.

It is by no means universally accepted that children go through a phase of separation from their parents and the consequent individuation. Scholars like Daniel Stern, in his book, "The Interpersonal World of the Infant" (1985), conclude that children possess selves and are separated from their caregivers from the very start.

Childhood traumas and the development of the narcissistic personality

Early childhood abuse and traumas trigger coping strategies and defense mechanisms, including narcissism. One of the coping strategies is to withdraw inwards, to seek gratification from a secure, reliable, and permanently-available source: from one's self. The child, fearful of further rejection and abuse, refrains from further interaction and resorts to grandiose fantasies of being loved and self-sufficient. Repeated hurt may lead to the development of a narcissistic personality.

Narcissistic Defense Mechanisms

Narcissistic defense mechanisms are a series of actions or reactions which tend to be enforced by a person, either consciously or unconsciously, to attend to their desired eventualities. A narcissist or a person suffering from narcissism will want certain situations to pan out the way they want, and certain relationships to be exactly what they desire and they would want their selves to be the most important factor in any circumstance. Not delving into the traits of a narcissist, since it is a subject that warrants a long discussion, here is what the various narcissistic defense mechanisms are.

One of the most common narcissistic defense mechanisms is repression. In most cases, the repression is unconscious but if a person is aware of his or her narcissistic personality, he or she may consciously repress many things. Repression can be of facts, emotions, situations, or expressions.

There are various forms of repression of which the most pertinent and also the most dangerous or unhealthy is the repression of another person. Repression of everything associated with the person or the relationship the narcissist has with the person is a way to repress the individual in totality. A narcissist would seldom repress another person partially. Narcissism leads to absolutism and the unconscious or conscious repression may become absolute in no uncertain terms

Another very common narcissistic defense mechanism is denial. A narcissist would be in denial of everything that he or she doesn't consider to be in their best interest. If there is anything that they don't like, don't wish to accept, or simply want to reject, there will be conscious denial on the part of the narcissist. Unconscious denials also exist but to lesser degrees. In most cases, repression is mostly unconscious but denial is almost always conscious. These are natural narcissistic defense mechanisms that will be prevalent in anyone who has any iota of narcissism in him or her.

Distortion is also one of the more common narcissistic defense mechanisms. One would indulge in distortion of facts, exaggeration of emotions or realities, minimization of grave situations to enforce their superiority or pseudo righteousness, and would also indulge in blatant lying in the process.

projection is also a common narcissistic defense mechanism. Using this potent weapon, a narcissist tends to seek control of someone else. In most cases, it is blame or enforcement of guilt on the other person.

How To Deal With Narcissistic Projection

When a narcissist projects their insecurities and self-doubt onto someone else, it's called narcissistic projection. This can be a defense mechanism that people with NPD use when they feel their inner insecurities or external image is being attacked. If you're on the receiving end of this behavior, it can be frustrating and even hurtful. But there are some things you can do to deal with it.

First, try to understand where the other person is coming from. They may be projecting because they feel insecure about themselves. If you can empathize with their feelings, it may help defuse the situation. (Defuse it to get away)

Second, don't take it personally. It's not really about you, it's about them. They will project onto another all of their thoughts and behaviors. If you have a strong sense of self it will be really helpful in seeing through this behavior.

Third, stand up for yourself. If someone is constantly putting you down or making you feel bad about yourself, it's important to speak up. Stand up for yourself and let them know that their behavior is not acceptable.

Lastly, don't enable their behavior. If you accept the projections, they're never going to learn to deal with their insecurities. So set boundaries and don't allow them to treat you poorly.

Why Do Narcissists Use Projection?

Narcissists use projection as a defense mechanism. Projection is when someone takes their thoughts, feelings, or behaviors and attributes them to someone else. This can be done in an attempt to distance themselves from their negative qualities or to make themselves seem more positive than they are.

Narcissists often project their feelings of insecurity and inadequacy onto others. They may do this in an attempt to make themselves feel superior and in control. Narcissists may also use projection as a way to avoid taking responsibility for their actions or to manipulate and control others.

If you are dealing with a narcissist, it is important to be aware of their use of projection. Be prepared to deal with their gaslighting attempts as the narcissist accuses you, they will attempt to make you believe it. You may need to set boundaries and communicate assertively to protect yourself from their manipulative behavior.

If a narcissist is a drug addict, alcoholic, or cheating then they will project it onto you to avoid accountability for what they are doing. Since narcissists are compulsive liars then they will project their lies onto you to make you look bad and to gain sympathy from others. Narcissists use projection as a way to shift the narrative away from their behavior and place their faults onto another.

If you are getting a divorce, they will project their issues onto you through the court, by lying to their lawyers, or a child custody evaluator. If they are being investigated by the IRS, they will project their financial issues onto you. Narcissists use projection as a way to deflect their problems and place the blame on someone else.

Projection is a common defense mechanism that we all use to some degree. However, narcissists use it excessively and in harmful ways. This is also known as narcissistic abuse.

CHAPTER EIGHT
HOW TO OVERCOME DEFENSE
MECHANISMS THROUGH THERAPY

You don't need to know all the fancy names for this or that defense. Intellectual understanding will only take you so far. The key is learning to recognize your defense mechanisms the moment you employ them. But the tricky thing about psychological defense mechanisms is that they are, generally speaking, unconscious. So how do you make the unconscious conscious?

Defense mechanisms tend to disrupt two essential life areas: intimate relationships and careers. If job after job and/or relationship after relationship keeps fizzling for no apparent reason, this suggests you are likely getting in your way by being defensive. Another way to recognize your defensive tendencies is to pay attention to the feedback of those closest to you.

Your habitual defense mechanisms are likely apparent to everyone but you. So when your loved ones suggest you may be stuck–and especially if you find their feedback distressing or offensive–it's worth taking a step back to re-evaluate. A defense mechanism is a learned self-protection device. It's an automatic, knee-jerk response. The key to letting go of these insecure habits is to become more secure. True security is attained by becoming more self-aware, and more mindful. Before you can accept yourself as you are, you first have to see yourself as you truly are.

Therapists are trained and experienced in working with their client's defenses. A skilled therapist can help you become more aware of your defenses, but at a pace, that feels right for you. You can't simply get rid of your defenses in one fell swoop like ripping off a Band-aid. A therapist can help you gently explore your defensive patterns, leading you to evaluate certain life areas in which these patterns may be holding you back. The aim isn't to let go of all your self-protection strategies. Rather, it's about making these strategies conscious. The goal is to intentionally decide when you need to protect yourself versus when it might benefit you to remain more open and vulnerable.

When Defense Mechanisms Interfere with Therapy

Our tongue is a powerful muscle. Human beings have learned to utilize language to love, comfort, destroy, and even protect our emotions.

Defense mechanisms can arise at any moment when we feel challenged, or perhaps when someone hits a nerve by speaking a truth that we may not be ready to hear or deal with in life. I define defense mechanisms as unconscious thoughts that trigger behaviors and reactions to avoid uncomfortable feelings, situations, and emotions.

For therapist and client, both may be triggered by something that is said or a nonverbal cue that may seem misleading. I encourage us to acknowledge that our emotions are valid, and we should never be judged for having a human reaction. Yes, even therapists at times say something they wish to forget was said in a session. When this does occur, I believe that this moment presents the perfect opportunity to pause, take a deep breath, and truly reflect on how to process our feelings.

It is important to note that is not your responsibility as a client to ensure that your therapist is not being triggered by your reaction, but counselors are human. In addition, the space that we are honored to hold for clients takes on many shapes and forms during a session, because we are constantly trying to align our thoughts with yours to understand how to best meet your needs.

The intimacy that exists between therapist and client within a counseling session can feel awkward and intimidating. There are usually two individuals in the room trying to utilize our best language skills to deepen an interpersonal professional relationship, all while trying to avoid feelings of judgment and shame within a session that may arise.

Within this communication dynamic, vulnerability often becomes the catalyst for a defense mechanism. At any given moment, there exists this strange window of opportunity for our defense mechanisms to come forth when we don't feel secure or safe.

DEFENSES AND WAYS A THERAPIST MAY GO ABOUT GETTING PAST THEM TO HELP THE PATIENT.

When one goes to a surgeon, for example, to remove a lump, the patient recognizes they have a lump and agrees to have the surgeon remove it. With a psychological problem, however, patients may recognize that they have some problem, but they often do not see it as a result of their life strategies (defenses or personality styles), and in trying to protect themselves with these defenses, patients may sabotage their therapy.

Even if they do have some insight into their maladaptive use of defenses, patients often show resistance to changing their life strategies. They would prefer that things go smoother in the world using the same life strategies they have been using up to now. Patients may seek validation of their style from the therapist or even advice on how to make their maladaptive defenses work better. Can you imagine a patient with a lump telling the surgeon to remove the lump but at the same time trying to convince the surgeon why it is better to live with the lump?

This is where the unconscious nature of defenses, and the resistance to changing one's defenses, comes into play. Resistance is often unconscious in patients as they may provide many rationalizations on why their maladaptive life strategies are valid. This resistance may occur even in the face of significant psychosocial troubles arising from these defenses as seen from the outside. The work of the therapy needs to overcome these barriers.

These maladaptive life strategies have been used by the patient both in past and present relationships, so it is no surprise that these personality styles will also manifest in the relationship with their therapist. It is the therapist's challenge to find the common thread that runs through the patient's interpersonal style and then guide the patient to use new and more adaptive life strategies.

The therapist attempts to remain neutral in attitude and does not disclose personal material to the patient. In this way, therapists try to keep their countertransference issues out of the session. Thus, the therapist and patient can begin to create a picture of the patient's personality style without undue influence of the therapist's style. If the patient's insight is poor and/or their defenses are of a certain quality that leads to dissatisfaction in the therapy, the defenses themselves can sabotage the help the patient needs to fix their defenses.

1. Consider the "Depth" of an interpretation

One common element consistent among various authors is Freud's original proposition from "The Interpretation of Dreams", identifying the primary goal of psychoanalytic work as making the unconscious conscious. Through the employment of interpretation on the part of the therapist, it is believed that patients can understand their typical ways of defending, thus rendering the defensive processes more controllable and less automatic and bringing these processes into their conscious awareness.

The first technique in this process is "clarification" to allow patients to verbalize and elucidate their defensive function without addressing any underlying meaning or unconscious process at work.

At this point, therapists confront or draw attention to the operation of what patients are doing during therapy; however, no deeper unconscious material (e.g. wishes, fantasies, or impulsive urges) would be included in the therapist's interpretations until a more thorough understanding of the unconscious conflict that underlies the defense is evident.

The second technical task in this process involves more profound exploratory work that is achieved through interpretation, which is considered essential to changing problematic defensive patterns in patients.

The surface-to-depth idea can also be used to organize the order in which the therapist uses therapeutic techniques. For instance, when working with patients diagnosed with personality disorders, the therapist should structure their strategies accordingly from surface to depth with "lighter" interventions such as questions and clarifications before moving on to interpretive work to give the patient enough time to assimilate understanding in a step-by-step approach.

The responsibility of the therapist to address defensive behaviour does not end at confrontation. The next step in dealing with defences is the action by which deeper understanding and insight help patients give up formidable defenses for more adaptive ones. Interpretations are used once the more unconscious material is better understood by the therapist and takes precedence over confrontations after that point.

2. Intervene with patients' most prominent defenses

The second principle suggests that therapists should confront more prominent defenses when they are obvious, significantly when these defenses obscure important repressed material.

Essentially, because all individuals use a multitude of defenses in any given psychotherapy session, therapists should focus on those defenses that seem to be most closely related to conflicts associated with symptoms, anxiety, presenting problems, or other difficulties associated with functioning. Furthermore, therapists should address characterological defences and those "out of character" because they are also most likely related to a symptom.

3. Interpretations should begin with defenses used as resistance

Another principle found was that therapists in psychodynamic psychotherapy address those defenses seen specifically as resistance in session.

Resistance is defined as any defensive process that interferes with the natural unfolding of therapy and thus prevents the further exploration and elaboration of unconscious material. Although resistance is defensive because it keeps specific affects, thoughts, ideas or impulses from consciousness, this construct is generally used when discussing the therapeutic setting.

The concept of defense is broader than resistance since resistance is a treatment function that takes meaning from the analytic process". Thus, while patients can use various defensive techniques in everyday life, they are only classified as resistant when these processes occur within the context of therapy. Freud clearly made this distinction by stating that "defensive mechanisms directed against former danger recur in the treatment as resistance against recovery".

4. Attend to defenses used both inside and outside of the therapeutic hour

The fourth principle refers to the difference between those defenses used within the therapeutic hour, which includes defenses used in the session, not about resistance, and those that patients recount from their everyday lives. Therapists should acknowledge when "reality-based" problems are influencing the defensive behaviour of patients. Current sources of stress (outside the therapy) and their interaction with personality needs and defenses be addressed before therapy can unfold productively. This implies that what unfolds outside of therapy is of value, and understanding the defensive processes that patients recount from their "outside" lives could be an equally valuable pursuit in-session.

This is in line with the suggestion that events from outside the therapeutic hour should be acknowledged and dealt with before systematic intervention focusing on defenses in-session is undertaken. Stressful life events could make patients appear more "defensive" in session than their typical personality suggests.

An example of this situation would be if a patient describes using the defense of splitting in their everyday life, but no evidence of splitting is observed during the session; the therapist must hence choose whether or not to make this part of the therapeutic work and to address it. Once externally based problems are under control, patients may be able to manage their inner world. This is the only way for patients who suffer from substance abuse problems or are diagnosed with personality disorders to benefit from therapy.

5. Consider the timing of interventions

The question of timing is an essential aspect of psychodynamic techniques concerning interpretation. Many, if not all, texts that aim to educate practitioners regarding approach use invariably discuss the intricacies involved in choosing the correct timing when formulating one's hypothesis about the patient and then vocalizing it during the therapeutic hour. This issue of timing can be divided up into two subcategories.

First, the global idea of timing examines when to focus on patients' defensive functioning over the entire therapy. This would include both shorter and longer therapy durations. The second aspect of timing is choosing the right moment within the session to interpret.

Concerning the more global idea of timing, therapists should address defenses in the middle phase of long-term therapy so that the alliance has had sufficient time to develop before the more uncovering and slightly more anxiety-provoking aspects of defensive behaviour are pointed out. Early interpretation is neither helpful nor harmful. However, early performance can damage the alliance and should be avoided when possible. Similarly, therapists should wait to address defenses too late in therapy as there may not be sufficient time to work through the material and thus may be more harmful to patients. Although defenses are "focused on" during the middle phase of therapy, they should be interpreted throughout therapy.

There needs to be more work aimed at understanding the issue of when to interpret during a psychotherapy session. The beginning is the most appropriate to allow enough time for patients to process the information. However, suppose patients are on the verge of gaining insight regarding their defensive behaviour.

In that case, the therapist may aid the process with an interpretation regardless of when this occurs during the session. Implications for practice and empirical evidence: Many psychodynamic psychotherapy training manuals teach this principle by getting trainees to judge when the patient is "ready to hear" certain conclusions the therapist wishes to share. Therapists should be aware of patient readiness, place in the treatment (i.e., early, middle, late), and timing during the session.

Additionally, applying this principle would depend on the type of psychodynamic therapy a clinician is practising, as it will determine how and when a therapist should address defenses. For example, working within an intensive short-term dynamic therapy model, therapists would interpret reasons much earlier in the process of therapy and with more frequency and intensity (e.g. the 'pressure and challenge' technique)

6. Avoid using technical language in interpretations

There is little debate regarding this principle, some agree that therapists should refrain from using overly technical language in their verbalizations to patients regarding defense mechanisms. Not surprisingly, no sources were found that endorsed the use of lengthy or technical terms in interpretations. Official objection to technical words was nearly unanimous in the psychoanalytic community.

The use of overly technical language by therapists may promote the use of intellectualization and isolation defenses by patients. These defense mechanisms share the function of distancing patients from the experience of the aspect. As a result, therapists who use overly verbose and technical-sounding interpretations may promote weak dosages in psychotherapy.

However, in some instances, when this approach is not providing the desired effect in the therapy, a more authoritative language may be used to overcome forces of repression.

CONCLUSION

Defense mechanisms are a way to protect oneself from being harmed by the world. We as humans need to have some kind of defense mechanism in place so we do not become completely vulnerable and hopeless when faced with challenges, because then they will feel impossible to overcome. A lot of people use their defense mechanisms without even realizing it – maybe you're guilty of this too! Going over these different types can help us be more aware of how our brain operates and what is going on around us at all times. This knowledge can be used positively or negatively depending on your perspective; either way, understanding them better should make life easier.

Defense mechanisms are a natural part of human psychology. They help the mind to cope with uncomfortable and traumatic situations or even emotions. However, some people routinely use defense mechanisms as a way of avoiding their feelings and emotions or excusing their behavior. This can hurt a person's mental health and even relationships.

If a person is continually relying on all the unhelpful patterns of thinking, they may wish to seek support from a qualified therapist. With the right treatment, people can reduce their use of defense mechanisms and then learn to address their feelings and emotions in a more positive and even constructive way.

We welcome questions or comments.

Please contact me or visit my Website:

Suzanne M. Howard
suzhoward@yahoo.com
www.suzannemhoward.com

If you enjoyed this book and you think it will benefit others, please take a few moments to write a review on your favorite store, and refer it to your friends.

REFERENCES

https://www.berkeleywellbeing.com/coping-mechanisms.html

https://www.sciencedirect.com/topics/psychology/coping-mechanisms

https://www.igi-global.com/dictionary/coping-mechanisms/56736

https://pediaa.com/what-is-coping-mechanism/

http://changingminds.org/explanations/behaviors/coping/coping.htmL

https://sintelly.com/articles/common-defense-mechanisms-and-why-we-use-them

https://www.e-therapy.uk/articles/what-are-defence-mechanisms-and-why-do-people-have-them

https://relationshipsrelearned.com/defense-mechanisms-simple-reasons-we-use-them/

https://www.mindbodygreen.com/articles/defense-mechanisms

https://www.google.com/url?sa=t&rct=j&q=&esrc=s&source=web&cd=&cad=rja&uact=8&ved=2ahUKEwiS09e4sbT7AhVpbKQEHetxAfA4FBAWegQICBAB&url=https%3A%2F%2Fwww.linkedin.com%2Fpulse%2Fwhat-type-defense-mechanisms-do-you-use-daily-basis-aware-garcia&usg=AOvVaw0bZZBgfNDD9W7MaWiNXOMB

https://rdcastro1.wordpress.com/2011/12/06/mental-health-ego-defense-mechanism/

https://www.google.com/url?sa=t&rct=j&q=&esrc=s&source=web&cd=&cad=rja&uact=8&ved=2ahUKEwiHwpPZmL7AhWO_7sIHdRxAVk4bhAWegQICBAB&url=https%3A%2F%2Fopenaccesspub.org%2Fijpr%2Farticle%2F999&usg=AOvVaw197sAuQWOkmHt6qWO6BK6D

https://quillbot.com/courses/effective-learning-strategies/chapter/chapter-16-managing-your-mental-and-physical-health/

https://quizlet.com/141264302/mental-health-terminology-and-defense-mechanisms-flash-cards/

https://openaccesspub.org/ijpr/article/999

https://www.fatherly.com/love-money/defense-mechanisms-that-can-hurt-relationship#:~:text=The%20Defense%20Mechanism%3A%20Denial

https://www.psychologytoday.com/us/blog/fulfillment-any-age/201706/the-5-defense-mechanisms-can-sabotage-your-relationship

https://www.healthyloveandmoney.com/blog/top-6-defense-mechanisms-impacting-your-relationship-and-finances

https://www.betterhelp.com/advice/defense-mechanisms/the-splitting-defense-mechanism-how-it-can-damage-your-relationships-without-you-knowing/

https://www.harleytherapy.co.uk/counselling/defensiveness-relationships.htm

https://relaysd.com/news/hearing-loss-denial-can-hurt-relationships

https://crowntowncounseling.com/wellness-articles/2017/2/8/relationship-destroyers-the-four-rs

https://medium.com/the-partnered-pen/defense-mechanisms-used-in-toxic-families-68b5c0a7d9a4

https://www.babyboomers.com/article/the-defense-mechanism-most-toxic-for-your-relationship/5b21bd84e4b0cce987aab7cd

https://www.7thsensepsychics.com/stories/dropping-your-defense-mechanisms-in-relationships/

https://www.worldsbest.rehab/narcissistic-projection/

https://thenarcissisticlife.com/narcissistic-projection/

https://unfilteredd.net/8-examples-of-narcissistic-projection/

https://www.interviewarea.com/frequently-asked-questions/is-projection-a-symptom-of-narcissism

https://narcissistblog.online/9-reasons-why-narcissists-use-narcissistic-projection/

Cramer, P. (2000). Defense mechanisms in psychology today: Further processes for adaptation. American Psychologist, 55(6), 637.

Dollinger, S. J., & Cramer, P. (19901. Children's defensive responses and emotional upset following a disaster: A projective assessment. Journal of Personali~ Assessment, 54, 116-127.

Farberow, N. L. (19801. Indirect self-destructive behavior in diabetics and Buerger's disease patients. In N. L. Farberow (Ed.), The many faces of suicide: lndiret self destructive behavior (pp. 79-88). New York:

McGraw-Hill.

Fulde, R., Junge, A., & Ahrens, S. (19951. Coping strategies and defense mechanisms and their relevance for the recovery after discectomy.

Journal of Psychosomatic Research, 39, 819-826.

.

www.ingramcontent.com/pod-product-compliance
Lightning Source LLC
Chambersburg PA
CBHW051629120626
46551CB00014B/1998